IRISH REPUBLICANISM

GOOD FRIDAY & AFTER

Daltún Ó Ceallaigh

Published by
Léirmheas
P.O. Box 3278, Dublin 6, Ireland

© Daltún Ó Ceallaigh, August 2000

ISBN 0-9518777-7-1

Politics - Law - History - Ireland

Printed from camera-ready copy and bound by
Elo Press Ltd, Dublin, Ireland

CONTENTS

Introduction		5
1.	Background	8
2.	The Good Friday Document	20
3.	The Irish Left	51
4.	Social Classes & Politics	68
5.	The International Context	80
6.	The Roots of Irish Neutrality	95
7.	Modern Republicanism	132
Notes to Chapters		147

INTRODUCTION

Clearly, an assessment of the contemporary meaning and future potential of Irish republicanism is now called for. The Nineties have seen the end of insurrection by the ('provisional') IRA and the emergence of Sinn Féin as a significant political force both north and south, and to one degree or another. Moreover, the Good Friday Document has set an altogether new framework for the development of politics on this island. At the same time, there are voices saying that these events do not mark an advance but a retreat for republicanism, while others claim that the consummation of nationalist history has been reached. Wherein lies the truth?

Naturally enough, we allocate a fair amount of space to evaluating the Good Friday Document. Although it is composed of eleven Parts, our focus in this is book chiefly on the first five and to the extent that the core question of sovereignty arises - i.e. the Declaration of Support, Constitutional Issues, and Strands One to Three. Other matters regarding individual and community rights, and so on, are being dealt with adequately elsewhere by experts in those areas.

Insofar as republicanism is a politics critical of the establishment generally, it is also necessary to place it in the overall scenario of the Irish Left wherein, we suggest, it could become the ballast as a truly radical force. This is not least owing to the increasingly centrist nature of the SDLP and Labour Party and the demise

Introduction

of Democratic Left, and because radical means going to the root of issues as republicans are prepared to do.[1]

However, the Left cannot just be approached by way of reflecting on organisation and policy, while taking for granted certain socio-political assumptions. There is a need at the beginning of the 21st century to carefully re-examine the sociological realities and political possibilities with which it has to cope and which should inform its ideas and methods. As a result, we update and expand some of the research and interpretation in this sphere which we first did nine years ago.[2]

Next, consideration is given to the international dimension. The changes here have been immense over the past decade ranging from the collapse of communism to the extension of the European Union. There are also the continuing transformations which have occurred politically, socially and culturally of a global character. All these are of course not without their impact on Ireland and have to be weighed up in that respect.

Because of the importance of the tradition of neutrality in Ireland, a chapter is devoted to this particular aspect of international relations. It is especially needed owing to the often unperceived depth of this tradition and a lack of appreciation of its several facets.

---

[1] From Latin *radix, radicis* for *root*.

[2] *Labour, Nationalism and Irish Freedom*, Daltún Ó Ceallaigh, Léirmheas, 1991.

Introduction

We conclude by trying to sum up what constitutes modern Irish republicanism and to gauge the prospects of its input to the life of our country in the new century and millennium. In doing so, we are not attempting the last word, but hoping at least to contribute to a debate.

But before proceeding to Good Friday and after, we should put where Irish republicanism stands now in recent historical and political context. While what follows in the next chapter cannot currently be proved in its entirety, one way or the other, we believe that it describes the basic position that developed over the past quarter of a century and more.

1. BACKGROUND [1]

The period of turbulence that is now hopefully drawing to a close began with the police assault on the Belfast office of Sinn Féin in the election year of 1964. An IRA military campaign had ended in 1962 and republicans were trying to promote their cause politically. The attitude of the northern authorities was to send the RUC into a staunchly nationalist area to seize a tricolour from a campaign office window, thus provoking the Divis Street riots. Two years later, the reconstituted UVF began to assassinate Catholics [2] and petrol bomb Catholic schools and premises. This was not in reaction to any nationalist political advance but, on the one hand, to the audacity of nationalists in celebrating their tradition upon the fiftieth anniversary of the 1916 Rising and, on the other, to Terence O'Neill's cosmetic gestures of cross-community reconciliation. The latter were also seen as a reflection of hated ecumenism. In addition, the work of the Campaign for Social Justice, established in Dungannon in 1964, was no doubt resented for its highlighting of anti-Catholic discrimination.

Next, in 1967/68, the police obstructed the nascent civil rights movement and ended up batoning its demonstrations to the ground. Then, in 1969, in Derry and

---

[1] This chapter and the next as well as the final one are based on a lecture given to the Ireland Institute in October 1998.

[2] John Scullion and then Peter Ward, both in June 1966.

Background

Belfast, they joined with loyalist thugs in assaults on nationalist flats and housing estates, employing their guns and armed vehicles to help kill nationalists in their homes or have them burned out.[3] The first bomb attacks of the 'troubles' in the north had already taken place earlier in the year, mainly at major electricity and water supplies.[4] These explosions, blamed on the IRA, were in reality the deeds of loyalist paramilitaries who used the classical fascist tactic of destroying some of their own facilities and blaming the enemy. By 1970, the British Tories were in power and they promptly sanctioned, and lent their army to carry out, the onslaught on the lower Falls (involving the notorious curfew) in which working class homes were smashed to pieces in the alleged search for arms.[5] Also in 1970, i.e. six years after this escalating terror commenced, the 'provisional' IRA uprising began.

In the past three decades, the nationalist community has experienced sectarian assassination, paramilitary and State torture, police-army shoot-to-kill activity, framing and imprisonment of innocent people, and 'security force' collaboration with loyalist death squads.

---

[3] Not how the Scarman Tribunal summarised it, yet for evidence see vol 1 of its report, pp 15-16, April 1972 (Cmd 566).

[4] A Catholic church was first bombed on 21st March; on 30th the electricity station at Castlereagh was so attacked; as for water supplies, the bombings were - 4th April Dunadry, 20th Silent Valley serving Belfast, 24th Lough Neagh likewise, and 25th Annalong.

[5] This author, a civil rights worker at the time, saw evidence of fireplaces pulled out, toilet bowls destroyed and holy statuettes in smithereens - all supposedly to uncover weapons.

Background

(Much of this has effectively been verified subsequently, either by the British themselves through reluctant inquiries and legal reviews or by international courts.) And, as the Irish Government knows, British Intelligence colluded with loyalists in bombing Dublin and other towns in the south, thus massacring civilians there.

Some commentators today file sympathetic reports about unionist objections to being asked to share power in a 'liberal democracy' with parties 'having private armies'. The fact is that 'Northern Ireland' is not and never has been a democracy, liberal or otherwise.[6] It is an arbitrary and violent colonial construct whose repressive laws were the envy of apartheid South Africa along with which country it had the distinction of being a one-party regime, albeit for the longer period of over fifty years.[7] Secondly, unionists had an army of their own from partition up to the Seventies, until the British took it away from them. The B-specials were the paramilitary wing of unionism of a part-time amateur kind, while the RUC were largely so in a full-time professional capacity when they were not engaged in attempts at crime prevention. Both were used as instruments for unionist persecution of nationalists. Indeed, Professor Brendan O'Leary of the London School of

---

[6] How it may now be assessed transitionally after the Good Friday Document is considered in the next chapter.

[7] South Africa once responded to criticisms of its repressive legislation by saying that it would gladly trade it for the north's Special Powers Acts.

Economics has written: "The outbreak of armed conflict in 1969 was partly caused by an unreformed, half-legitimate police service, responsible for seven of the first eight deaths." [8] Furthermore, the IRA is not a 'private' army in the sense of what attaches to a mobster or a drug baron. It is an outgrowth of a harassed people, a significant section of which endorsed the response of armed struggle.

On the latter point, the hypocrisy of some anti-republicans in regard to ascertaining the will of the people was brought out with the rise of Sinn Féin. When republicans were reluctant to participate in elections within a colonialist framework, even tactically, the anti-republicans in question dismissed them as a small bunch of misfits with no base among the people and afraid of a ballot, which they constantly dared them to submit themselves to. Then, when republicans changed their tactics and went up for election in the north, the result for these persons was such a shock that the voters were next dismissed as either ignorant or merely lodging a protest without endorsing the republican project. It is not difficult to see who was really exposed in this way.

As the Nineties approached, the north was in a state of political paralysis and the IRA campaign had been going on for almost twenty years. That campaign had included attacks on the RUC, UDR (later RIR),[9]

---

[8] 'Opinion', *The Irish Times*, 28/7/00.

[9] Ulster Defence Regiment, then absorbed into the Royal Irish Regiment.

Background

mainstream British forces, property, and civilians (both deliberately depending on their role and, otherwise - usually according to statements afterwards - accidentally). Assaults occurred in the north, in Britain and elsewhere.

The reaction of the British to this offensive varied. They were not especially worried about RUC and UDR/RIR losses, particularly at the levels involved. There was of course more concern about the British army, but it was not composed of conscripts and the rate of loss was not sufficient there either to generate an outcry in Britain. Civilian casualties (what a British general would call 'collateral damage' when inflicted by his own forces) produced public abhorrence - more when they took place in Britain than in the north - yet, of themselves, did not really move the British establishment significantly towards disengagement. Striking at property probably had most effect, either when it led in the six counties to a charge on 'UK' funds or, more notably, when the locale was Britain and it both disrupted daily life and again produced sizeable monetary consequences. In the latter instance, the refusal of insurance companies in London to cover fully for damage caused by explosions at the city's financial centre had a substantial impact;[10] the linked fear of international financial institutions pulling out of London intensified anxiety in this connection.

---

[10] Leading, among other things, to the Reinsurance (Acts of Terrorism) Act 1993.

Background

While not all facets of the so-called 'troubles' thus disturbed the British greatly, the cumulative result of the state of affairs, according to a widely held belief, was nonetheless to create a weary desire in the British establishment to extricate itself from Ireland. In different ways, this was said by unionists, SDLP representatives, Alliance figures, and some British politicians, including conservatives. (Of course, no really important British establishment figure could articulate this openly - except obliquely in speeches and interviews or inadvertently in foreign newspapers or the like [11] - and those in official positions had to sometimes disingenuously profess the opposite.) The new context of the post-Cold War world also helped in lessening even further any strategic worries (never wholly absent, despite claims to the contrary) about pulling out of the north. International embarrassment was also an influence.

Moreover, 1990 was not just the year of the famous Brooke speech about Britain having no "selfish, strategic interest" in the north. It was also when a British defence review called *Options for Change* was carried out. This was mainly a cost-cutting exercise strongly encouraged by the Treasury. There is reason to believe that, around this time, certain mandarins there and in the Ministry of Defence came to the conclusion that the north was too costly and diversionary to hold onto,

---

[11] As Patrick Mayhew did once when being interviewed by a German newspaper.

Background

would have to be relinquished, and have been working to that agenda ever since.

The apparent evolution of a disengagement mentality was not altogether surprising. It is unlikely that there would have been a Sunningdale accord with limited power-sharing and a Council of Ireland, for what they were worth, had there not been a revolt emanating from the nationalist ghettos. And the Anglo-Irish Agreement was clearly a reaction to the rise of Sinn Féin in the early Eighties.[12] But neither of these initiatives succeeded in stabilisation and the turmoil continued.

On the specifically military front, the British political, if ironically not always the military, reaction was: firstly in the Seventies that the IRA could be defeated; then in the Eighties that it could be isolated; and finally in the Nineties that it had to be brought on board. By that stage the British had implicitly recognised that for them the long war had become the wrong war. Or, as it has also been put, the position was one of stalemate, not checkmate.[13] The lesson once more was that a guerrilla army is successful, not when it is victorious, but when it cannot be defeated. It is at the point when this is recognised that its enemy accepts the need to negotiate and compromise.

---

[12] Among other sources, see Garret Fitzgerald, *All in a Life,* Gill & Macmillan, 1991. The New Ireland Forum of 1983 was similarly inspired.

[13] An interviewee in *'Bandit Country' - The IRA & South Armagh,* Toby Harnden, Hodder & Stoughton, 1999.

Background

However, the British still did not reach the stage where they were prepared actually to issue a declaration of intent to withdraw, never mind go in fact. And it seemed that they felt themselves incapable of even beginning to proceed to that denouement while the IRA campaign endured. Too much loss of face would have been entailed. Therefore, the situation became stuck at a point which it did not appear possible to go beyond.

It has been argued that the dirty war of the British in the Eighties (shoot to kill etc) and the loyalist murder campaigns finally demoralised republicans and that is really why *they* sued for peace. However, that is a distortion of historical reality. Rather is it that republicans had come to accept the emergence of a withdrawal mentality in Britain along with the political difficulty of it being brought to fruition by the British establishment while there was military conflict. Moreover, the IRA never expected to actually defeat the British in a purely military fashion. The view then developed that an IRA war of attrition followed by a British declaration of intent to leave and then a formal departure was too simplistic and that the process would be more complicated and less obvious, but nonetheless continue to move in the right direction.

This perspective was bolstered by the electoral breakthrough of Sinn Féin in the early Eighties. If that could be consolidated and extended, the case and excuse for British disentanglement from Irish affairs once and for all would be greatly strengthened. This was so

Background

against the backdrop alluded to above where the British had clearly already disengaged from Ireland psychologically; unionists were perceived by them as an anachronism and annoyance, and there was no wish otherwise to maintain a presence on the island. Thus there seemed little point in nationalists continuing to be at risk of the attacks, although they had not broken their will, launched by British terrorists and loyalist murderers. The latter factors, therefore, were ancillary, not determinant. In the overall scheme of things, IRA bombs in England had more of an impact than British undercover work in Tyrone.

An important element in putting pressure on the British to depart is also the policy of the Irish Government. But this had become watered down in the previous two decades, mainly as a result of the violence, to seeking an influence in the administration of the north rather than demanding a withdrawal by Westminster. Public attitudes in the south had also become confused and, while not abandoning nationalism, as opinion polls confirmed, were somewhat muted in their active demand for British disengagement. This was probably again because of the violence, especially when this involved IRA 'mistakes' and civilian casualties. Indeed, the essentially bigoted and intransigent character of unionism was often shielded by the publicity and sympathy engendered by such 'mistakes'.

What republicans had then to consider was how to break the logjam through best exploiting any underlying trend in the British establishment to get out, and therefore how to rally public and political support in Ireland and abroad for that objective. This would involve as well placing unionism once more fully on the defensive as it had been in the late Sixties in terms of its antediluvian and intolerant character. (Major's growing parliamentary difficulties did not facilitate a disengagement tendency, but they did not eliminate it, as unionists obviously feared.)

A not insignificant influence on the republican psyche was also the information emanating from the 1991 census in the subsequent two years. This appeared to suggest that, in a decade or so, there could be a nationalist majority in the electorate of the six counties. Previously, this seemed an impossibility owing not only to fertility patterns, but discrimination and emigration, which were now being tackled. While northern majority consent to unity cut across republican principle, if it could actually be achieved as a means to reunification, it could hardly then be objectionable in practice.[14]

Since the Sixties, political events in the north had thus gone through two main phases. The first was the civil rights movement; the second was the IRA campaign. (In the latter period, the SDLP may have been the larger of the two nationalist parties, but an undefeatable IRA and a growing Sinn Féin still determined the pace of events for the British, first by the attempts

---

[14] The points in this paragraph are dealt with more in the next chapter (pp 33-37).

Background

to subdue or marginalise republicans and then to include them.) By the mid to late Eighties, the need for republicans to reflect on a third stage embracing all nationalists began to be addressed. The idea therefore developed of a nationalist alliance stretching throughout the north, down to Dublin, and across to the US, with solidarity being encouraged in Britain and anywhere else possible in the world, particularly in places such as Australia where there were large Irish populations. Moreover, it was understood that insofar as militancy would continue, it should be more of a mass character, and residents' groups were to become significant in this regard.

In summary, the strategy assumed that the British were ready to compromise, but were unwilling or unable to do so while military confrontation persisted. It also rested on the belief that the rise of Sinn Féin and a cessation of violence were necessary but not sufficient conditions to make them finally sit down and talk meaningfully about a totally new situation. What was also required was mobilisation of the people in the north, before the nation and in the face of Britain and the world. And all this had to be in the context of building, here and abroad, what some people came to call a 'pan-nationalist front'.

Although the rhetoric of the establishment suggested that a ceasefire would not be enough to have everybody participate in talks and there would have to be a public forswearing of violence for all time and a handing up of arms, the likelihood was that these stipulations could not be politically insisted on in an environment of peace. This was because they would be viewed as dogmatic and unrealistic and putting the ceasefire at risk.

Moreover, the republican position would also be bolstered in that peace would prevail at the same time as unionists would probably try to sabotage new discussions (as they did) and thus be seen to be unreasonable and destructive. In addition, the revisionist case for the Irish State distancing itself from the cause of national independence would be virtually undermined against this backdrop. To do so would be politically untenable and morally reprehensible.

Of course, history has many twists and turns and Major's domestic political difficulties and the block of decommissioning led eventually to the breakdown of the first ceasefire. However, the undercurrent towards a settlement reasserted itself with the advent of Blair and stability at Westminster, and led to the events of Holy Week 1998. But how far did the latter fulfil the expectations republicans had of the peace process? It is this question that we now consider.

2. THE GOOD FRIDAY DOCUMENT

Before the Good Friday Document, the six counties were an undemocratic, illegitimate and failed political entity, and after it they remain so. The Document is a testament to that. Its special provisions for power-sharing in the Executive, checks and balances in the Assembly, measures against discrimination, and an all-Ireland Ministerial Council confirm the true nature, status and dysfunctionality of 'Northern Ireland'. Nowhere else in 'these islands' and almost nowhere else in Europe can such distinctive arrangements be found.[1] And all this is not surprising. It follows from what Professor Joe Lee of UCC constantly reminds us:[2] that 'Northern Ireland' was created by naked force against the will of the Irish people in general and northern nationalists in particular, and on the basis of seizing the largest amount of territory which unionists could safely dominate, irrespective of the wishes of the local inhabitants, most markedly in counties such as Fermanagh and Tyrone.

So, does the Good Friday Document nonetheless open up possibilities for progressing the republican cause?

---

[1] The obvious comparisons are Belgium and Switzerland, but even their constitutions do not go as far as the Good Friday Document. The recent constitution of Bosnia-Herzegovina (the Dayton Accord) is the closest example and that speaks for itself.

[2] In several of his articles in *The Sunday Tribune* over the past few years. See also Chapter Note 1, p 147.

The Document commences with a Declaration which is largely rhetorical, yet useful in setting a tone of hope, initiative, reconciliation and commitment. The Declaration also goes beyond this in one Paragraph to confirm the interlocking and interdependent character of institutional and constitutional structures, such as the Assembly and the all-Ireland Ministerial Council, a point which is repeated and emphasised elsewhere in the Document.

Then it proceeds to Constitutional Issues. Among other things, this Part calls for recognition of "the legitimacy of whatever choice is freely exercised by a majority of the people of Northern Ireland with regard to its status, whether they prefer to continue to support the Union with Great Britain or a sovereign united Ireland; ... " It goes on to say that "it is for the people of the island of Ireland alone, by agreement between the two parts respectively and without external impediment, to exercise their right of self-determination on the basis of consent, freely and concurrently given, North and South, to bring about a united Ireland, if that is their wish, accepting that this right must be achieved and exercised with and subject to the agreement and consent of a majority of the people of Northern Ireland; ... " Next it requires acknowledgement that "the present wish of a majority of the people of Northern Ireland, freely exercised and legitimate, is to maintain the Union and, accordingly, that Northern Ireland's status as part of the United Kingdom reflects and relies upon that wish; and that it would be wrong to make any change in the status of Northern Ireland save with the consent of a majority of its people; ... "

This view of consent and self-determination is impossible for a republican to accept; to do so would amount to political abjuration and ideological suicide. Gerry Adams summed up the appropriate reaction at the reconvened Ard Fheis of Sinn Féin in May 1998 when he said: "When the vote was taken [on the Good Friday Document on that day in 1998] I did not vote ... " and "We do not accept the legitimacy of the six county statelet. And we never will, ... " This is because, as he later indicated, it "rests on the gerrymander of partition and is thus a violation of the principle of democracy and a denial of the right of the Irish people as a whole to freely resolve their own destiny. We held, and hold, that Ireland is the valid constituency for mapping out the future of the people of the island, and without external interference. However, it is not feasible to proceed in that way immediately, not least because of the attitude of the British government. So, we must see how we can advance the position without a negation of principle. No other party has been asked to abandon its philosophy and analysis. Nor will we abandon ours and there is nothing in the Document which compels us do so. There is no affirmation or action required in it which can be construed as binding one to the Document's flawed definition of self-determination."[3] Seeking the endorsement by republicans of this section without qualification is like asking unionists to subscribe unreservedly to the Declaration of Independence of 1919.[4] In particular, the reference to the absence of "external impediment" is belied by the imposition of bifurcated ballots and majorities on the Irish people.

In response to Gerry Adams' speech, Labour luminary Dick Spring was characteristically first out to defend the unionist veto and suggested that all those who had voted "yes" had definitely endorsed the pseudo-self-determination of the Good Friday Document.[5] Bertie Ahern had not been much better when he came on television after the referenda to say that the Irish people had accepted partition, but then this may be true enough for the leadership of Fianna Fáil. In fact, to portray the votes of 22 May 1998 as an instance of self-determination by the people of Ireland is an attempt at a massive exercise in public deception along the lines of Joseph Goebbels that if you tell a lie, tell a big enough one and tell it often enough, especially through mass media, it will come to be believed through a process of sheer mental weariness. The conflict in Ireland

---

[3] Address to American Irish Historical Society, 27/5/98. Also G Adams: " ... the referendums do not constitute the exercise of national self-determination" (press conference 7/5/98); " ... self-determination for the people of this island has yet to be achieved" (Ard Fheis 8/4/00).

[4] Some commentators see in this aspect of SF statements "contrary indications" to positions otherwise, see Chapter Note 2, p 147.

[5] *Parliamentary Debates*, Dáil Éireann, 28/5/99.

has been about the establishment of a sovereign, united, all-island State. Yet, that was the one option not put to the people in the superimposed separate constituencies. Even the rabidly anti-republican Eilis O'Hanlon had to admit that the vote was "one heavily circumscribed so as not to alarm sensitive orange souls; ... " [6]

John Waters spelt it out more fully. "It seems obvious to me that what happened on May 22nd was not an exercise in national self-determination. Such an exercise would have required the same questions about the nature of government on this island to be asked North and South, and would have been followed by a pooling of the results in both jurisdictions to provide a single answer.

"If May 22nd had been a genuine exercise in national self-determination, the British army would now be in the process of withdrawing from the North, because a majority of the Irish nation would have expressed a democratic desire for this to occur." [7]

Both Waters and even some other, less critical, media commentators have grasped that the Document does not have to be fully affirmed in order to be positively utilised. Mo Mowlam also effectively conceded this in the British House of Commons when she said that "most of the people will, in their heart of hearts, cherry-pick. ... no-one is signing up to 100 per cent,

---

[6] *Sunday Independent*, 21/6/98.

[7] 'Opinion', *The Irish Times*, 8/9/98.

..."[8] In fact, If there is a "right to seek constitutional change by peaceful and legitimate means",[9] there is also a logical right to adhere to an interpretation justifying such change, viz that 'Northern Ireland' is an unjust fabrication which should be superseded. It is in that light that the institutions and progressive constitutional opportunities in the Document should be taken advantage of as far as possible.[10]

The point about the defective nature of the referenda is brought out more specifically by reference to the situation in the twenty-six counties. The people there were deprived of the opportunity to choose among key elements of the Document (e.g. amendment of Articles 2 & 3 of the Constitution, on the one hand, and of Article 29 to establish a North-South Ministerial Council, on the other). The majority of people throughout Ireland who voted "yes" actually included many (probably most) republicans because of the further diminution in the Act of Union entailed in the Ministerial Council. It is thus impossible to deduce from such an affirmative result that everybody so voting accepted the unionist veto and the measure of British power that will continue to be exercised over the six counties in the

---

[8] *Hansard (House of Commons)*, 20/4/98. She reiterated this position at the subsequent British Labour Party conference, see *The Irish Times*, 1/10/98.

[9] Section on Rights *etc*, Paragraph 1.

[10] Even Séamus Mallon has pointed out that because he accepts that the status of the north cannot be changed without the consent of a majority there, that does not mean the he consents to that status (British-Irish Association conference, October 1994).

immediate future. Therefore, to say that those who continue to reject the veto and such British interference are thus going against the democratic wishes of a majority of the people of Ireland is an unsustainable argument. Indeed, many of them would then be accused in effect of going against their own vote!

In other words, in their anxiety to secure endorsement of the Document, the powers that be produced a state of affairs whereby they cannot soundly claim that all aspects of it, including key ones for them, have been agreed to. All that can be safely concluded is that a majority saw in the Document hopes of moving the situation forward. Probably, for some this meant assenting to the entire text, while for others it signified accepting only parts of it. But it will not be feasible to ascertain how many ended up in either camp. Such a vote cannot therefore be construed as a signal that the Document is generally viewed as a final settlement as distinct from an interim accommodation.

However, if a *coup de grace* were needed for the pretence of Irish national self-determination on 22 May 1998, it was given on 11 February 2000 when a British Secretary of State unilaterally, and thus against the wishes of nationalists and the Irish Government, suspended the main institutions set up as a result of the Good Friday Document.

And republican participation in the Assembly, Executive, and so on, is not an acquiescence in 'Northern Ireland's' legitimacy so much as a limited and realistic step taken in a transition towards national democracy and not without linkage to all-Ireland provisions.[11] A distinction should be drawn between the illegitimacy of the entity and the legitimacy of the exceptional arrangements (power-sharing etc) instituted for the conduct of public affairs. In other words, the first is confirmed by the second. Looked at another way, what is involved is a paradox of decolonisation. A military analogy would be to say that to parachute behind enemy lines is not to surrender.

Nonetheless, it has been alleged by dissident republicans that Sinn Féin is actually helping to implement British rule in the north. But that is false in more ways than one. Sinn Féin Ministers have had to take no oath of allegiance to the Crown (unlike their counterparts in Scotland and Wales); they give no other fealty to it; and they will implement no policy and perform no act (including flag-flying) which will serve to confirm or consolidate Crown rule. But there is day to day administration to be carried out in any form of polity under the headings of education and health, and so on. Children have to be taught to read and write; the sick have to be cared for. That has nothing essentially to do with Crown rule. But it is still better that in Ireland it should be done by Irish people. More generally, just as Sinn Féin Ministers will otherwise contribute to nothing in the Executive

---

[11] These also include the following yet to be established 32 county bodies: Parliamentary Forum, Committee on Human Rights, and Civic Forum.

to entrench British rule, neither will any Sinn Féin member in the Assembly.

In continuing to reject British interference in Ireland, it has also been alleged by some unionists that their presence is thus being rejected. That is not so now anymore than it was previously. There is no desire on the part of republicans to eject any native of Ireland or prevent whoever on the island wants to call him or her self British from doing so or from attempting to realise that attitude socially, culturally and politically by any legal and democratic means, including the holding of British citizenship. Repudiating British interference means opposing the exercise of power by the British Government and Parliament to any extent over any part of Ireland. Such power is a distinct fact and quite different from the rights and entitlements of unionists and those who choose to classify themselves as British.

However, while republicans cannot accept that the consent of a majority in the six counties is necessary *in principle* in order to bring about Irish unity, should it be achievable *in practice*, it is hardly objectionable as a means towards an end. Insofar as Irish unity is not going to come into being tomorrow, whatever about the diminution of British sovereignty over the north involved in the Ministerial Council, consideration ought to be given to how potentially to make progress towards northern majority consent. Some commentators purport to see this outlook as convoluted. However, there is nothing really complicated about it. A simple analogy will suffice. If something is stolen from a person and the offender can be induced to give it back, well and good. But that does mean that an offence has not been committed in the first place and that restitution is not needed. That is the basic situation regarding the national democratic rights of northern nationalists.

There are five headings that might be looked at in connection with seeking northern majority consent to unity:
- Persuasion of Unionists,
- Policy of British,
- Fertility of Nationalists,
- Emigration of Unionists,
- Immigration of Nationalists.

Persuasion of Unionists Obviously, one should continue the propaganda work of trying to convert, as far as possible, unionists to a classical republican position of accepting a secular (or at least pluralist)[12] national democracy in Ireland which could allow for devolution within the island. In this, they would be encouraged to take pride in themselves as citizens rather than languish in the status of subjects. That does not necessarily mean supporting the SDLP or Sinn Féin, in the latter case not least because of recent associations for unionists or reluctance to accept left-wing policies as

---

[12] The difference between secular and pluralist is that, in the first case, the religious has no public role, while, in the second, it is to a certain extent allowed one, along with the non-religious, such as in schools, but only on an equal basis.

well. But it does pertain to voting patterns in a plebiscite and that includes not voting at all which has been a notable feature of unionist electoral behaviour in recent years. In other words, some unionists may not vote for constitutional change, but resignedly neither vote against it.

A nationalist argument has always been that if the sectarian structures, laws and practices of the six-county statelet are dismantled, the main rationale for unionism will be removed which could open the way for unionists (or at least their offspring) to review their stance on reunification. Moreover, apart from the exaggerations of the past, the entity with which they would now be asked to link up is hardly capable of being portrayed any longer as priest-ridden and economically backward. There is also now no great overall difference in social welfare or living standards between north and south [13] and leaving the UK, when it occurs, need not have any negative impact in these areas.[14] Indeed, certain Irish social welfare rates are now sometimes better than in the UK.

These considerations could prove significant in diminishing repulsion towards and increasing acceptance of some form of Irish unity, especially in a context of

---

[13] On living standards, see Garret FitzGerald, 'Opinion', *The Irish Times*, 27/4/00.

[14] As for British subsidies, while the need for these could be overtaken by all-Ireland economic development, the British might well be prepared to continue them for a period after reunification in order to consolidate an end to conflict.

continually chilling relations between the British and unionists. There might also be the attraction, especially given the latter phenomenon, of having 20% influence in a united Ireland rather than just 2% in a united kingdom, not least for ambitious élites.

However, we have previously cautioned against simplistic economic reductionism which ignores other social and psychological factors in the formation or at least endurance of attitudes. That is to say, one cannot rely on persuasion alone, even in the changed circumstances that will hopefully flow from the Good Friday Document, to bring about Irish reunification. Persuasion of unionists must be pursued to the utmost, but it has to be augmented by political pressure.

Policy of British Just because the British have now legislated for the possible detachment of the six counties from the United Kingdom and their incorporation in a united Ireland, and have also declared themselves neutral on the issue, does not mean that they are thus inevitably bound to an allegedly neutral stance - a case of the British empire becoming the British umpire. (They are of course not objectively neutral through continuing to passively accept a unionist veto on full secession.) It is still open to the British in future to become active 'persuaders', and work should continue at all levels and in all countries towards getting a policy adopted by them in favour of (a) Irish unity and (b) measures to induce consent thereto. In other words, at least to resurrect in substance the 1988 British Labour Party policy which Mo Mowlam, among others, signed.

It could, in time, be argued again that Britain should, especially if unionists remain obstructionist, reconsider issuing a signal of an intention to depart and then proceed towards that objective, at first seeking to convince unionists to negotiate about the terms of unity and, if that failed, then drafting the repeal of all claims to jurisdiction over the six counties and opening discussions with the south about linkage of the north to it. In realistic terms, and given that military action is not envisaged in such a scenario, one would then require at least unionist acquiescence, if not eventual and reluctant consent. But that would not be an altogether unrealistic expectation in the light of a British policy as just described and the terms which might be offered, including decentralisation within Ireland.[15]

It may be said that the current British stance on a unionist veto on certain options is not consistent with the disengagement mentality which was identified by several nationalists as helping to lead to the peace process. The fact is, however, that even if the withdrawal tendency is there, progress on foot of it is not going to be linear. That is not the nature of politics. The British will continue to oscillate somewhat between ap-

---

[15] As it is, 79% of those polled in the north in 1999 have said they would accept a united Ireland if there was a majority vote for it in the six counties; only 16%, almost all Protestants, said otherwise (*Irish Independent*, 7/7/99). One wonders if these figures would carry over to acceptance of the British going if they said they actively wanted out.

peasement of unionists and satisfaction of nationalists, according to the exigencies of the moment. Moreover, on occasion there is the difference possibly to be drawn between appearance and reality in regard to what the British are up to in the longer term, such as when Blair talks about the Union lasting into another generation. The issue is whether, over time, and given the crests and troughs of political developments, the basic trend is upwards in the direction of unity. That depends significantly upon nationalists, because even if a disengagement tendency remains, it will lapse into dormancy in the absence of sustained nationalist activity.

Fertility of Nationalists The proportion of Catholics (in effect, nationalists), or those of that background, in the northern population at the last census in 1991 was estimated at 43% and it is thought to be about 45% now;[16] moreover, in '91, it was assessed to be around 52% in the -1 to 14 age cohorts. However, expert opinion is divided on whether it will ever exceed the 50% mark in electoral terms simply through natural reproduction and Catholics staying in the north or, if so, when.[17] And that is not surprising as one is talking about what are unpredictable human factors of fertility and migration. The qualification which is sometimes

---

[16] The informed speculation of some demographers regarding the outcome of the 2001 census. The combined SDLP and SF vote in the European election of 1999 was 45%, i.e. the proportion of those casting a ballot and not just of the population of all ages.

[17] See Garret FitzGerald's 'Opinion' articles in *The Irish Times* of 7/9/96 and 26/7/97. In the first, in particular, he refers to the 'Catholic' proportion of 1991 being down to 48.9% in the 0-1 age group.

made here about there being a significant number of pro-Union Catholics, we have demonstrated before to be a unionist chimera.[18] It has then been said that Catholic allegiance to nationalism will not always remain the same, but then it won't necessarily change either.[19] The conclusion is that reproduction may be a significant, perhaps the most significant, factor in the situation, but not necessarily adequate in itself. But demography does not depend on that alone.

Emigration of Unionists This has already begun to take place, especially among the middle-classes and particularly where children are going to Britain for third-level education and then staying there.[20] The propensity to emigrate to 'the mainland' might be strengthened for those unionists who cannot stomach the Good Friday Document and its full implications of equality in respect of identity as well as civil rights.[21] On the other hand, a decline in violence and the possible increase in prosperity could work the other way. But the question is

---

[18] *Reconsiderations of Irish History and* Culture, Daltún Ó Ceallaigh (Introd & Ed), Léirmheas, 1994 (p 23). See also my letter to *The Irish Times* of 29/7/97 in Chapter Note 3, p 148.

[19] There is also the worry expressed by unionist apologist Paul Bew: "how much is the economic success of the Celtic Tiger eating away at the material arguments for Catholic Unionism?", *Sunday Independent*, 28/11/99.

[20] It has been suggested by some educationalists that this is more a consequence of new arrangements for allocating places than the troubles. But, whatever the cause, the effect is much the same.

[21] Garret FitzGerald writes: "It is this annual disappearance of almost two-fifths of the better-educated unionist young people ... which threatens the majority position of Protestant unionism in Northern Ireland." 'Opinion', *The Irish Times*, 7/8/99.

whether this would be sufficient to eliminate the distance which many unionists obviously feel from a society in which the egalitarian is the norm and when the political and demographic balance is steadily shifting towards nationalists. Sometimes, internal migration seems the first step towards emigration. Dr John Dunlop, former Moderator of the Presbyterian church, has observed: "The trend whereby Presbyterians, along with Anglicans and Methodists, were no longer bidding for houses in many parts of Belfast was a tragic manifestation of demographic suicide ... " [22]

The provisions for preventing discrimination in employment and so on, and indeed redressing the sectarian imbalance in unemployment, could also diminish the rate of nationalist emigration and increase the rate for unionists insofar as, by definition, the latter will have less chance of getting a job in the north than would otherwise have been the case, assuming that a full employment situation is not round the corner. That is to say that the economic benefits of peace for unionists could be lessened by an intensified equality policy. A particular strain that will emerge here will be the disbandment of large numbers of unionists from the RUC, the prison services and private 'security' firms as those elements are both scaled down to an appropriate size in a post-conflict scenario and made more representative of the community.

---

[22] *The Irish Times*, 21/8/98. However, Dr Dunlop only mentioned "aggression" as an explanation.

Good Friday Document

There is no doubt that the morale of unionists *per se* has been seriously damaged by the peace process. Leading unionist dissident Jeffrey Donaldson captured this quite well when he said: "The sense of defeatism within unionism is palpable. We lack self-confidence and seem to work to an agenda which is about the management of decline within a political framework which is set by pan-nationalism." [23] The parades issue alone has had a disproportionate effect on them. The end or curtailment of triumphalist marches has brought home to unionists that the old order is crumbling fast. Another illustration of this despondent outlook was articulated by the Orange Order when it announced that "Ulster is in extreme peril with its existence under greater threat than at any time since the Home Rule crisis of 1912-14. Enemies within and without threaten unionism" which "is currently in some disarray." [24] This gives rise to the further speculation about how some unionists will ultimately react also to the new all-Ireland perspective - by accepting it or leaving the island.

Immigration of Nationalists Thought has not been given up to now to a feature which has operated elsewhere in the world to help alter the political balance of a situation and that is immigration of nationalists from the twenty-six counties, Britain and, to a lesser extent, elsewhere in the EU to the north, which could not be prevented under EU rules. This was originally a fear of

---

[23] *The Irish Times*, 14/7/98.

[24] *The Orange Standard*, September 1998.

unionists as regards the south, and was reflected prior to EU membership in employment legislation to prevent the green hordes from coming across the border.[25] Such immigration might also be encouraged from the US, Australia, and so on, although this may not be legally so straightforward in some instances. Up until now, such an idea would have appeared unrealistic, given the conflict in the north and its high unemployment rates. But if the latter two factors altered substantially and positively, the notion might no longer be so strained as it would have seemed previously.

The general phenomenon of the 'exiled' Irish, first generation or otherwise, returning to Ireland in the era of the 'Celtic tiger' is already well-established and seems set to continue. For all one knows, what we are referring to here in respect of the six counties may be already significantly under way. Studies and statistics in the years to come will prove interesting.

Finally, in regard to figures, the shortfall in a plebiscite on unity today might be about 56,500.[26] Naturally, one cannot assume the same turnout as in the example from which this figure is derived (1997 Westminster election) or that people will vote in a one-issue plebiscite along the same nationalist-unionist lines. However, this reference gives one some measure of what may be involved.

---

[25] Safeguarding of Employment Act 1947, repealed 1981.

[26] See Chapter Note 4 on page 149.

Moving on to actual constitutional changes, the three bases of British sovereignty over the six counties up to 1998 were the:

- Union with Ireland Act 1800 ('Act of Union'),
- Government of Ireland Act 1920,
- Northern Ireland Constitution Act 1973.

The second and most of the third have now been repealed and remaining legislation is subject to the Northern Ireland Act 1998 insofar as it has "effect notwithstanding any other previous enactment". Also, the Act in Part V reflects the amendments to the Irish Constitution which introduced new Articles 3.2 and 29.7 to allow for an all-Ireland Ministerial Council and Implementation Bodies.

These are the key legal differences over Sunningdale which left the Government of Ireland Act on the statute book and, at most, envisaged ordinary legislation in the Assembly and the Oireachtas regarding a Council of Ireland. What has happened now is that constitutional legislation has been introduced at Westminster and Irish constitutional amendments adopted to give powers to all-Ireland bodies. In other words, the Northern Ireland Constitution Act 1973 did not specify a Council of Ireland, while the '98 Act provides for a North-South Ministerial Council and linked Implementation Bodies; the Irish Constitution was not amended in 1973 to allow for the first, while in' 98 it has been altered to provide for the second. These steps would not be necessary if a partial cession of sovereignty to all-

Ireland institutions by the two governments were not being allowed for.

In 1922, and following the Treaty, Article 1 of the Act of Union was diminished by the Irish Free State Acts [27] in that the reference in the former to "Ireland" henceforth could legally only signify "Northern Ireland".[28] The Union had also thus clearly ceased to be "for ever after" as envisaged in the 1800 statute, with consequential ongoing implications for the north as well. Now the Act of Union has been further diminished, because British sovereignty over the *six counties* is lessened, albeit not eliminated, in view of the Ministerial Council. The analogy is the surrender of an element of sovereignty to the EU regarding its Council of Ministers.[29]

Section 1 of the Northern Ireland Constitution Act of 1973, which effectively reasserted sovereignty over the north, has also been repealed and replaced by Section 1 of the '98 Act. In addition to the limiting effect on the latter of the all-Ireland institutions stipulated elsewhere, the difference also is that secession of the six counties from the UK is now provided for in British constitutional law *and* with a view solely to incorporation in a united Ireland.[30] Prior to this, such a position was only con-

---

[27] *Agreement* and *Consequential Provisions* statutes.

[28] Trimble: " ... the 1922 Irish Free State (Agreement) Act. To that extent the Act of Union (Ireland) was modified ... " *Hansard (House of Commons)*, 22/7/98.

[29] See also Chapter Note 5, p 150.

[30] See also Chapter Note 6, p 151.

tained in a Communiqué (1973) and then an Agreement (1985).

This evolution should not be underestimated. It is legally almost unique. We do not know of another State in the world that has written into its constitution a provision for the secession of part of its territory and integration in another State. It may be that this development is not adequately appreciated, because it is allied to the demand for a majority vote in the six counties for actual secession. However, it might also be viewed as an incentive to try and achieve that vote as already addressed above.

Ian Paisley identified the most basic point following from the statement in the '98 Act that it was "notwithstanding any other previous enactment". During his speech to the House of Commons at the second reading of the Northern Ireland Bill he said: "That goes back to the 1800 Act of Union and before that. I should be delighted if the Minister [Paul Murphy] stood up and gave the lie to Bertie Ahern's statement in the Dáil, when he said that the British were now out of the equation because they had been content to do away with the 1920 Act and would introduce a Bill - this Bill - ... [that] would make all the other Acts subservient to it. An axe has been taken to the root of the Union." [31]

Despite what has been indicated above, Professor Paul Bew of Queen's University Belfast not only be-

---

[31] *Hansard (House of Commons)*, 20/7/98.

lieves that the Good Friday Document has shored up unionism, but that the Act pursuant thereto goes further than the Document in a unionist direction. This is based on a silly misreading of parliamentary drafting conventions in London. He has quoted in particular from what became Section 23 and reads: "(1) The executive power in Northern Ireland shall continue to be vested in Her Majesty. (2) As respects transferred matters, the prerogative and other executive functions of Her Majesty in relation to Northern Ireland shall ... be exercisable on Her Majesty's behalf by any Minister or Northern Ireland Department".[32] In particular, he is excited about the references to "Her Majesty".

In fact, these are on a par with the opening of every British statute wherein it is said that the measure is "enacted by the Queen's most Excellent Majesty ... ", while everybody knows that in reality one is talking about the House of Commons, with or without the eventual compliance of the Lords. All of this is quaint monarchical window-dressing not unlike the fatuous bowing and scraping to Elizabeth Windsor at official functions. When reading and listening to Professor Bew, one often wonders whom he is actually trying to convince - others or himself. The Orange Order, however, is not so sanguine: "The Republic of Ireland already has a greater say than ever before in the affairs

---

[32] 'Opinion', *The Irish Times*, 13/6/98.

of Northern Ireland, and if the Belfast Agreement is implemented in full that influence will increase." [33]

Finally, on the aspect of sovereignty, a word about the British-Irish Council (BIC) - what some people have called the 'Council of the Isles'. This was intended by the unionists as at least a counter to the North-South Ministerial Council (NSMC), and, preferably, the latter was to be subsumed under it. In fact, the BIC has a much more restricted remit and no attached Implementation Bodies. Furthermore, the NSMC is certainly not subordinate to it. Apart from that, unionists may end up with less than they still anticipated in the BIC when they find themselves sitting across the table, not only from northern nationalists and the southern Irish, but Scottish and Welsh nationalists and the less than loving English.

Grasping the true nature of what has been achieved in the Document in relation to sovereignty and the way forward is what led Gerry Adams to say elsewhere in a speech already referred to: "When I hear some wiseacres saying that the Good Friday Document is 'Sunningdale for slow learners', I think of the wee unionist woman who said recently that it was in fact a 'United Ireland for slow learners'." [34]

A further major difference of a political kind produced in 1998 over the situation twenty-five years

---

[33] *Op cit* (24), p 36.

[34] *Op cit* (3), 27/5/98, p 23, as she was originally quoted in a 'vox pop' in the newspapers.

previously was that republicans were to be part of the legislature and administration of the six counties as well as participants in the all-Ireland Ministerial Council. It may be said that this was not so a quarter century beforehand due not least to Sinn Féin's abstention from full-bodied involvement in politics. That may be true, but it does not alter a significant political contrast which has been passed over by several observers. Beyond that, there is also the internal constitutional progress that nationalists held only four out of eleven places in the Executive of 1974 as appointed by the Secretary of State, whereas they occupy six out of twelve posts in 2000 as of legal right. This advance from a 36% to a 50% position is very important.[35] What is also noticeable is that not all unionists are as resistant to the Ministerial Council as to the Council of Ireland of 1973 which suggests, at least and at last, a degree of resignation to the all-Ireland dimension.

Of course, there are those who may still argue that, whatever about differences in law between 1973 and 1998, there will not turn out to be much contrast between the two situations in day to day reality. Indeed, that is always possible, if one rests one's laurels there and does not follow the resultant state of affairs through with the necessary, continuing political struggle. By definition, a potential is just that and no more and can remain unfulfilled if the required action is not taken on

---

[35] It would still obtain even if there were just two parties, respectively unionist and nationalist.

foot of it. However, to begin with, one must be precise and examine the position at *all levels*, and anyone who suggests that, there has not been real constitutional change over twenty-five years ago and adheres to the 'Sunningdale for slow learners' interpretation simply does not understand the law and is historically inaccurate.

We now turn to the further amendments of the Irish Constitution in respect of Articles 2 and 3 and, in the course of that, formally record the positive influence which the pro-Articles 2 and 3 lobby have had on the amendments. But, firstly, it should be made clear that many of us in that lobby never adopted the stance that there should be absolutely no change in the Articles - there is always more than one way of saying the same thing. In fact, this author produced two republican redrafts in 1993 and '96 respectively.[36]

However, when the 'anti' lobby really got going just over a quarter of a century ago, the demand of some in that camp was for deletion of the Articles. That has not happened. Alternatively, they tried to reword the Articles in various ways which would have removed from them their national democratic content.[37] Let us consider the new wordings in that light.

---

[36] See *Sovereign People or Crown Subjects?* 1993, (pp 66-67) and *Britain and Ireland - Sovereignty and Nationality*, 1996, Léirmheas (pp 38-39).

[37] For example, the Workers Party *Eleventh Amendment of the Constitution Bill* of 1990.

Article 2 now effectively holds that there is an Irish nation which exists throughout the island of Ireland, even if there are also those on the island who either say they are not part of the nation or do not want to be so politically.

Article 1 (and this is important) remains unaltered and says: "The Irish nation hereby affirms its inalienable, indefeasible, and sovereign right to choose its own form of Government ... "

Article 3 gives up the claim by the Oireachtas and Irish Government to a right of jurisdiction over the six counties. (Ironically, the orthodox republican stance never recognised such a right of a 'Free State' parliament and administration.) The Article then goes on to envisage a united Ireland arising from consent of a majority of the people "in both jurisdictions". In fact, this is compatible with the principle that the valid constituency for determining the political future of Ireland is the island, while acknowledging the reality that the people are spread across two jurisdictions. It would have been different if the phrase in quotation was "in each jurisdiction", which was in earlier drafts leaked to the media, but changed in later ones.[38]

The reference to a "firm will of the Irish nation" to unity in the new Article 3 is also important and again links in with both the definition of the nation as existing throughout the island and the continuing mention in the

---

[38] See also Chapter Note 7, p 152.

Preamble about seeking to have "the unity of our country restored". It can be argued that there is thus still a constitutional imperative to strive towards unity.

In summary, Articles 1 to 3, as they now stand, assert that there is an Irish nation extending across the thirty-two counties with a right to sovereignty and can be construed as stating that the people of Ireland are entitled to establish a united Ireland by decision of a majority thereof. As already stated, if, in practice, that can be attained along with northern majority consent, well and good, but at least a principle has thus been upheld in the face of the six-county gerrymander.

Our belief is that, when current papers of State and of various individuals are opened up in decades to come, it will be seen that what has just been described would not have occurred had it not been for the pro-Articles 2 and 3 lobby. At the end of the day, and in all the circumstances prevailing, we would suggest that that lobby discharged its duty to its country with reasonable success.

We have argued elsewhere that the realities and rights of the situation in the north demanded that, on the issue of sovereignty, there had to be a constitutional compromise and that if one couldn't have a unitary Irish republic in the present, neither could one continue simply with a united British kingdom. Given the analysis we have put forward, there is now the opportunity to put that compromise into practice. Inevitably, there has had to be flexibility in the use of language and the employment of concepts, and some implications of the Good Friday Document have been left to be worked out. Of course that also means that the opportunity exists to renege on such a compromise if the political will falters. And there has been plenty of evidence of that danger since Good Friday 1998. However, should u-turns be attempted, that would be a recipe for disaster. It is to be hoped that, as we proceed, all sides will appreciate that measures will have to be implemented to construct a *via media* between traditional positions and that these measures should be adopted with a sense of give and take and in a spirit of sensitivity. We must all accept justice and none of us seek surrender.

At the same time, republicans should not undervalue the extent to which unionists have had to concede. They were determined that there would not be a power-sharing cabinet in the north, especially one incorporating Sinn Féin, whatever about an Assembly committee system. They were opposed to an all-Ireland ministerial council with a decision-making capacity, whatever about north-south co-operation. They did not want all-Ireland bodies with executive powers, whatever about some localised cross-border liaison.[39] They said they were now prepared for civil rights, but seemed far from ready for the equal rights, inclusive of

---

[39] "It could be said that the weapons imbroglio has distracted attention from the establishment of embryo structures for all-Ireland government in certain areas of public life." Deaglán de Bréadún, *Irish Times*, 20/2/99.

the cultural, which are now on the way (note their carping about the union jack being the only proper flag to fly over the Assembly - in fact, there is generally none). They demanded an end to the Anglo-Irish Agreement, but it has simply been recast as the British-Irish Intergovernmental Conference.[40] In all of these areas, they have been obliged to give, although republicans would naturally have preferred to have had a wider *initial* scope of responsibility incorporated in the all-Ireland dimension. Nonetheless, it is particularly evident that what has been achieved is far in advance of the 'reformed Stormont' perspective of some in the Sixties.

As a last ditch hope, some unionists ruminate about the possibility of common economic and social concerns as well as progress on the equality front making people forget about constitutional issues and perhaps leading to a restructuration of northern politics simply along social democratic-conservative lines.[41] Of course, it is the British constitutional link which is to be forgotten about, while remaining. Yet another form of wishful reductionism, albeit coming from an unusual source. But the general lesson of the beginning of the 21st century is that nationalism does not fade that easily. Nor should it, because it is a matter of identity and dignity,

---

[40] "The role of the Irish state formally in the intergovernmental conference is as strong as in the Anglo-Irish Agreement ... Informally its involvement in the process of implementing the positive [Good Friday] Agreement continues to increase." (Todd, *op cit*, end of Chapter Note [2] 2, p 148.)

[41] For example, Duncan Shipley Dalton of the UUP at the Irish Association on 29/10/99. According to some journalists, he has been dismissed by unionist colleagues as an Englishman not to be taken seriously!

and the autonomy that ought to go with it. If unionists think that northern nationalists have grown strong and confident only to abandon an essential *raison d'être*, they can think again.

Besides, what is not sufficiently queried is how far the changes in question might lessen the significance of a united kingdom for unionists which is no longer a buttress of supremacist Britishness, thus leading *them* to be attracted to the benefits of a united Ireland referred to earlier. At the psychological and ideological levels what would then also be needed is a development and strengthening of a sense of civic Irishness within which varieties of cultural (including Gaelic) Irishness could continue to exist. Whether or not, over time, some kind of civic-cultural convergence would then occur, only history can tell.

The task now is to harness the dynamic of the situation and advance nationalist entitlements to the limit within the framework of the Good Friday Document and through securing the Bill of Rights that it allows for. And such rights, it has to be underlined, go beyond the older agenda of individual liberties and include the full nationalist ethos. In due course, there should be a reassessment of progress towards the ultimate objective and the further way forward in that direction. However, the termination of armed struggle does not necessarily mean the end of popular defiance. It is not impossible that what may still occur in the future is civil resistance, if the pledge to accommodate nationalist rights is not fulfilled or at least insufficiently so. The choice lies with the unionists and the British.

However, apart from what has just been said, it would be irresponsible not to observe that a frightening spectre hovers over the Good Friday Document. If the promise of Easter 1998 is not fulfilled, there are those who may not be content with civil resistance and may resort in disgust at the political process to all-out insurrection and with ferocity. The signs already are that these will not just be ageing republican dissidents, but a new generation which will tolerate no further procrastination on basic human rights, including those of nationality. Expectations have been raised and republicanism has once more entered into the mainstream consciousness of youth. Some of them could, in frustration, turn to militaristic organisations which will not be easily expunged by renewed censorship or draconian laws. It would be a terrible tragedy if our children felt impelled to resort again to violence. That must not be allowed to happen.

3. THE IRISH LEFT

The 'Left' is an ambiguous term. It dates from the period leading up to the French Revolution when, in the Estates General, the nobility sat on the King's right and the 'third estate' [1] on his left. This seating was perpetuated in the post-revolutionary national assemblies with radical democrats and liberals occupying the latter position vis-à-vis the parliamentary president. It also became the norm in other legislatures in the 19th century and was in time to include socialists.[2] So, from early days, the term covered a number of political stances and could be said to define more what one was not than what one was - i.e. not of the aristocracy or of what later became known as the establishment, insofar as the latter was generally either derived from the *ancien régime* or conservative.

The first question that has to be posed in the modern world is: should the Left now be taken as a synonym for socialism?

The Left might be construed as involving more than socialists insofar as it can continue to cover all forms of opposition to the conservative establishment. Thus liberals, in the Irish sense, who are against restrictions on personal liberties ranging from private morality to civil rights could be considered on the Left. The Greens would be viewed by some as on the Left to the extent

---

[1] Effectively, the bourgeoisie or middle classes.

[2] As the Left gained power, the positioning changed in some cases.

that their environmentalism often pits them against the establishment. But others and several of the Greens themselves would regard that party as unique in a way that we shall examine below. In a sense, therefore, the difference between the narrow and broad interpretation of Left is essentially whether or not one defines it by reference only to rigorous democratic and liberal positions, which would include socialists, or also by reference to radical social and economic principles, which would exclude non-socialists.

Those principles for a socialist are that the production of goods, services, and wealth, because they are the result of a communal process, ought to be subject to social control. There is also the moral criterion of 'from each according to ability, to each according to need'. Of course, that leaves a wide range of policy choices from nationalisation and centralisation to mere taxation and expenditure measures, with many intermediate combinations being possible such as co-operatives, and so on. Also, left-wing opinions vary on the proper nature and extent of social welfare provision. Socialists further look behind policies to see what class interests inspire them.[3] Moreover, they have a sense of struggle which entails ongoing, incremental change until a final goal is achieved rather than satisfaction with short-term results. And struggle means not only in the 'external' world, but also within the movement itself

---

[3] For more about social classes, see next chapter.

through a constant critique of social analysis, political strategy, and immediate demands.

Non-socialists, however, do not accept that communal process should lead to social control. At the extreme, they ignore the inherited nature of wealth and how it was obtained originally as well as other contemporary and challengeable means of acquisition. They wish to see the State just holding the ring as the market then works out demand and supply, and the distribution of income. The imbalance in power which employers have in the productive system is not regarded as undemocratic so much as the luck of birth or the return for enterprise and risk-taking. Again, there are modifications of this non-socialist position, which have been adopted either from a philosophical or a political point of view, in the latter instance usually where compromise has proved necessary with the rise of socialism. Principles of inheritance and private property may remain intact, but be qualified so as to curb what are seen as excesses sometimes attaching thereto. As for welfare services and benefits, non-socialists may accept these, but are likely to take a minimalist view of what is necessary. They also portray class concerns as the general interest and see stasis rather than transformation as the normal structural condition of society.

Given the spectrum which exists within socialism and that which also is to be found within capitalism, there is thus the argument that they can overlap in practice. After all, it was Bismarck who introduced social welfare and Lange who argued for the social market.[4] However, overlap should not be confused with convergence and for two reasons. To begin with, the first is by definition partial, whereas the second suggests total fusion - i.e. leaving no meaningful areas of distinction. Moreover, even where there is overlap in practice, differences remain as to what is a principle in a crisis situation. For example, if there are problems with the social market, what is more sacrosanct - the social or the market? In other words, is the market not to be unduly interfered with or must the social dimension prevail?

In fact, it does not really matter which of the above definitions of the Left one uses, providing it does not confound the adoption of a fully progressive strategy. That is to say, one can either think of the Left as signifying socialist and then go on to identify parties within that category, after which one also seeks to build alliances with wider democratic forces on appropriate issues such as civil liberties, and so on. (Those using this approach then sometimes utilise 'Progressive' as the overarching rubric.) Or one can conceive of the Left as actually including both the socialist and the radical democrat and liberal, which still leaves room for the same differentiated levels of co-operation. It is our judgement that, in Ireland, people tend generally to mean socialist or social democratic when they say 'Left' and, therefore, we shall employ the term in that sense and then

---

[4] See also Chapter Note 1, p 159.

go on to consider the Left's involvement with other progressive forces.[5]

The party political organisations of significance, to one degree or another, that would have been named outside of Labour as definitely on the Left in Ireland until recently were, in order of size: Sinn Féin, Democratic Left, the Socialist Party, and the Communist Party. With regard to size, Sinn Féin was more significant than Democratic Left throughout the thirty-two counties in terms of elected representatives, although it was behind DL in that respect in the Dáil; at the same time, it had a higher rating in opinion polls than DL in the twenty-six counties. DL, however, is now out of the party equation through absorption into Labour. The Socialist Party is on a par with Sinn Féin in the Dáil (one deputy each), but behind it in the opinion polls in the south and has no representatives in the north. The Communist Party is included, not because it has any representative presence or is likely to acquire one, but owing to a continuing, albeit declining, influence in the trade union movement and a certain intellectual input to the Left as well as being a facilitator of contacts within it.[6]

---

[5] Left with a small 'l' is of course used as a relative term in regard to policy positions in all parties; therefore, even Fine Gael is supposed to have a 'left' and 'right' wing.

[6] The latter two aspects are reflected in the James Connolly Education Trust.

But what of the Labour Party and the SDLP (the meaning of whose initials is rarely spelled out [7]). In the first instance, few would now aver that the Labour Party is socialist in any radical sense or is likely to become so. The question is whether, despite its title, it is currently even social democratic as distinct from centrist. The latter difference is between a party which at least is economically interventionist, strongly welfarist, and fiscally redistributive, and one which is more qualified in those respects because, in its would-be social base and vote-getting potential, it wants to be what some political scientists designate as 'catch-all'. As for the SDLP, while there are at least some social democratic elements within it, that organisation is really a modernisation of the old Nationalist Party - a fairly conservative, middle-class organisation of northern Catholics, while Sinn Féin is generally the radical, working class manifestation of that community. The SDLP may be in the Socialist International; however, that is about as Left as it gets.

As for the Greens, some would see them as conservative in an older and more positive sense in that they look askance at industrialisation or, at least, the form that it has taken. In contrast to a tendency in socialism, they are more inclined to seek harmony with nature than master it. Also, several of them would be wary of social control in ways that many socialists would not be; there is often as much a sense of the in-

---

[7] Social Democratic and Labour Party.

dividual as of the community among Greens. In Ireland, they are also euro-sceptical and opposed to military alliances. Yet again, it has to be said that there is not just one sort of Green anymore than there is a single type of conservative or socialist and thus various combinations and emphases of position can be found. In fact, we believe that, in the modern political world, the Greens are somewhat *sui generis*. But there is certainly scope for the Left to co-operate with them.

What then are the prospects for the Left in Ireland? The Labour Party, although it will continue to have its ups and downs, is likely to simply endure at much the same strength as now. Even the adhesion of DL has not changed that as is evident from the 1999 local elections and opinion polls since then. The result of combination has proved to be less than the sum of the two parts. It may be a while, if ever, before the floating vote returns to it as in 1992. Typically enough for such a vote, ephemeral factors were at work then rather than any great political-ideological shift in Irish society. The sleaze of Fianna Fáil, the lacklustreness of Fine Gael, the competence, moderation and integrity of Labour in opposition - all came together to render the latter as an alternative for the protest vote.

However, Fianna Fáil has now got a second chance in the eyes of some people under the leadership of Bertie Ahern, although how long that will last is another matter as tribunals trundle on. Moreover, FF still plays the populist card on nationalist and social issues quite well. Fine Gael's spell in Government resuscitated that party somewhat. Otherwise, Labour still appears to some people as largely the political voice of the trade unions, even though many of their members remain loyal to Fianna Fáil through the populism referred to, while others are put off by Labour's indifference or hostility towards nationalism. (In fact, in the course of the LP-DL merger, it has now formally proclaimed itself as "post-nationalist", a trendiness which may boomerang in Irish circumstances.) [8]

It is worth pausing here to consider this last characteristic of Labour which has an intricate pedigree. There has been a tendency in world socialism from its early days which is antagonistic to nationality and stems from the assertion of a false opposition between internationalism and nationalism. In reality, the first, when genuinely pursued, is based on the second. Nationalism, as the expression of the freedom of nations, is hostile to imperialism (the real antithesis of internationalism) and is in no way incompatible with the democratic co-operation of nations, for example through the UN. The point has, however, become clouded by both conceptual and terminological confusion whereby Hitler, for instance, is classified as a nationalist when, in truth, his ultimate aim was not the emancipation of Germany from Allied domination but the subjugation of other na-

---

[8] As I have written elsewhere, post-nationalism confuses limitations on sovereign power with the end of the nation *per se* (see *op cit* (36), '96, p 44). It also tries to bypass the nation by appealing to the region, but we await the first regionalist martyr.

tions. The idea of the international working class has also been used to attack nationality when there is actually no conflict between being loyal to things distinctively national and, at the same time, recognising class interests across frontiers.

It is significant that these forms of 'left-wing' anti-nationalism first emerged among some metropolitan socialists whose own countries' nationality either never, or no longer, was in question. For example, some of the anti-nationalist views one hears in the Irish Labour Party today would have been quite congruent with those of Rosa Luxemburg. However, some thinkers on the Left, especially in colonial countries, eventually began to counter this ideological deformation and Connolly was a harbinger of them; although, many in the Labour Party would regard him as more of an aberration. In his own day, and under Orange influences, leftist anti-national attitudes were articulated against him in the person of William Walker.

At a purely pragmatic level, Labour has always had difficulty with the national (or constitutional) question because of its perceived divisive potential among the working class on the island. The response has then often been one of simple evasion or a return to a Luxemburg-type anti-nationalism as an ideological justification for the failure to deal with an awkward but real issue that just won't go away. The latest revelation of this propensity is the naïve and wishful assertion that the national question has been overtaken by the Good Friday Document and that the way is now open for Labour to advance unimpeded by that question to become at least the second largest party in the twenty-six counties. Thus, politics there are to be brought into line with the alleged left-right standard of the rest of Europe.

In fact, the Good Friday Document is only the beginning of the contemporary albeit, hopefully, final phase in tackling the national question. Ironically, the left-right 'normalisation' of Irish politics, for which Labour so much yearns, will continue to be delayed by the inability to understand this reality. It remains the situation that only when the national question is truly solved will such normalisation have a chance of occurring. (Labour's difficulty with nationalism is probably also the underlying explanation for its persistently erroneous claim to be the oldest political party in Ireland, when that distinction actually attaches to Sinn Féin.) [9]

Returning now to the overall left-wing perspective, the Socialist Party is an interesting new addition to the main political scene. But this Trotskyist splinter from Labour is unlikely to go beyond mopping up some working-class discontent here and there which can find no other local expression. The Communist Party will continue performing the educational and contact roles ascribed to it above, but does not seem to have any other future. It never really had much of a chance in Irish political culture and has even less of one now in

---

[9] See also Chapter Note 2, p 159.

the wake of the exposés in eastern Europe with which some people, even if unfairly, associate it.

The only new manifestation on the Irish political landscape which is likely to be of importance is a resurgent Sinn Féin which also happens to be the sole, significant all-Ireland group in the list of the Left. There is no question about its securely established position in the north. The main organisational issue there is whether or not it will actually overtake the SDLP, which it has a fair possibility of doing, although not to the point of entirely displacing it. In the south, it is set to grow for a number of reasons.

Firstly, it is now the only real alternative to the left of Labour for those who want to vote that way, especially when Labour goes into coalition with Fine Gael (and now possibly with the PDs according to Ruairí Quinn). Moreover, it is more rooted in the lower working class in some areas than Labour. This aspect will intensify insofar as Democratic Left has now disappeared into the LP.[10] Indeed, the electoral mobilisation, as in the north, of persons who were previously non-voters may prove particularly crucial. Its other main strength is that it is the only genuine and progressive nationalist party in Ireland and will appeal to people in varying degrees across the social spectrum on those bases. Fianna Fáil could be at notable risk in this regard, not least insofar

---

[10] "The demise of Democratic Left would create a great chance for Sinn Féin to replace them as the most radical urban party, ..." Ronan Fanning, 'Who's behind this DL-Labour merger?', *Sunday Independent*, 9/8/98.

as the possible reabsorption of the PDs would fuel right-wing socio-economic policies and dampen nationalist sentiment within it.

Previously, the national-progressive option was not there. Instead there was just the verbal republicanism of Fianna Fáil,[11] the effectively enduring 'Commonwealth' outlook of Fine Gael, and the indifference-to-antagonism towards nationalism of Labour (all the while rummaging around ostrich-like for a non-national way).

However, up until the present, Sinn Féin could not benefit from this situation in the context of its gagging under Section 31 [12] and the negative impact of ongoing violence. But that has changed and both Sinn Féin and its leadership's qualities now have a standing in Irish politics which will likely pay dividends in the years to come. In fact, the process has already started with the significant rises in the Sinn Féin vote throughout Ireland at the last general, European and local elections, particularly in the twenty-six counties and especially locally there in 1999.[13]

Overall support for Sinn Féin in the twenty-six county opinion polls has sometimes placed it as the fourth largest party after FF, FG and LP at 4 to 5%. An

---

[11] See also Chapter Note 3, p159.

[12] ... of the Broadcasting Authority Act 1960 whose ministerial use denied it publicity on radio and television.

[13] The point about the general and local elections in the twenty-six counties relates to particular areas or constituencies as SF went up only in a select few. On the other hand, it did go forward in all euro-constituencies in '99 and got 6.33% of the vote. For further details, see Chapter Note 4, p 160.

interesting survey of youth in July 2000, however, revealed that, of those aged 18 to 24 years, 14% would vote for Sinn Féin.[14] (Not surprisingly then, Sinn Féin has the fastest growing youth wing of any political party.) Earlier in the month of July, another poll representative of adults in every age cohort showed the most popular party leader to be Gerry Adams with an approval rating at 61% and 3% higher than Taoiseach Bertie Ahern.[15]

But all this is not to say that Sinn Féin is going to become the largest party or even another Clann na Poblachta. Yet, given our finely balanced political system, it would take no more than the five or six Dáil seats which it is possible for Sinn Féin to get (inclusive of its present one) in order to make it a significant player in national politics. That is why it is increasingly accepted by analysts and in the media that Sinn Féin could be in government in Dublin in the not too distant future. There have been novel coalitions before, but one including a party which is both solidly left and authentically republican would be without precedent and have a dynamic of historic proportion.

Lastly, the policies of the Left in the new century have to be considered. It is not feasible here to go into all the details of possible programmes. That would require a book in itself. However, the lessons of past so-

---

[14] MRBI survey in *The Irish Times*, 27/7/00. FF scored 22%, Greens 8%, FG 5%, LP 5% and PDs 3%. No opinion was voiced by 14%.

[15] *The Sunday Tribune*, 9/7/00.

cialism have to be learned. The central one of those is that principle must be combined with flexibility without becoming opportunistic pragmatism. That of course is easy to say, but can any more specific guidance be given as to what that means?

The guiding perspective should be that of economic democracy and the social economy. A vibrant public sector will continue to be needed. But we should not see the issue in polarised terms of nationalisation or privatisation. Those options will remain in certain cases and will be joined by that of public-private partnerships (PPPs). Beyond that, employee and community involvement in economic management and financial return are necessary as well - that is, *socialisation*. A range of possibilities can be imaginatively explored from employee share-holding to profit sharing, from worker directors to joint ownerships. It can also demonstrate that there need be no contradiction between economic efficiency and social justice. At the same time, we have to be aware that, while capitalism has transformed itself in many respects, its essential driving force has not ceased to exist. And that is to make the most profit at the least cost in wages. Employees still need trade unions and a political party of the Left to defend their distinctive interests.

Two dominant criteria should be adhered to in drawing up government policy - national planning and equality of opportunity. Planning must at least entail an overview of society and the economy, and the setting of appropriate objectives, as well as create incentives or make interventions when need be. And this is not incompatible with a market mechanism and freedom of choice. Equality of opportunity must underlie action and policies in housing, health, social services, and income distribution.[16] It should also lead to enhanced investment in education and training and in recreational facilities, which are especially germane to that greatest and most abundant resource of all - our youth. Young Ireland has a new and vibrant meaning in the 21st century and must be fully catered for.

But if the young constitute the majority of the population, we should not forget that women in particular make up around half of it. Yet, for all the progress that has been recorded in women's rights over the past thirty years, there is much that remains to be accomplished. Here, let us highlight two fundamental points. Firstly, the International Convention for the Elimination of All Forms of Discrimination against Women should be fully incorporated into Irish law as a standard of reference for what has already been done and what is outstanding. Secondly, Article 41(2) of the 1937 Constitution which, in essence, states that a woman's place is in the home, should be amended. Moreover, women working at home ought to be supported by appropriate taxation and income policies. When working away from home, creche facilities need to be rendered adequate

---

[16] See Chapter Note 5, p 161.

and affordable.[17] (That is not to say that the latter two points should only concern women, but that the immediate social reality is that they are likely to impinge on them more than on men.) But these are only some of the steps that ought to be taken to protect and promote the interests of women in Ireland today.

The Left must also emphasise that it firmly includes the cultural as being important to the all-round good of people. In Ireland, a gauge of its relevance to the particular circumstances of this society will be its attitude and policies towards the Irish language, given both the value of that tongue and the pressures it is under. But some radical thinking has to be done here as well. For example, are resources best utilised in translating all statutes into Irish, and so on, as distinct from advancing Irish in an everyday environment so as to touch on the lives of the greatest number of citizens?

If Irish had really been established as the first language of the nation, then a legalistic attitude would be understandable. But, taking account of the facts on the ground, why not use the law and expenditure measures to encourage more of a Gaelic ambience through more widespread use of bilingual signs and general communications, for instance? Tax incentives could further be introduced to promote the use of Irish in these and other ways in the private sector. These are only a couple of illustrations which are inspired by an approach of social osmosis whereby people can be instructed al-

---

[17] These policies are already those of Sinn Féin.

most subliminally and painlessly in the language to a degree. Education at every level, including adult, will continue to be crucial but, again, innovation and imagination should be the hall marks of the efforts concerned. The employment of the full range of information and media technology must underpin all of these policies.

Going back to the broader scenario, many other issues and dichotomies require to be addressed in the political, economic and cultural spheres, and from different angles, such as: development and the environment, the family and the individual, tradition and modernity, initiative and reward, solidarity and dependency, privacy and openness, crime and justice, freedom and responsibility.

In all of these tasks, structures of regeneration will also be important, both by way of new ones and taking advantage of the voluntary associations of civil society which are already in existence.

In summary, what is demanded is a politics of emancipation which balances the personal and the communal so as to achieve the maximum well-being of both.

4. SOCIAL CLASSES AND POLITICS

A term that can create confusion nowadays is 'working class', not to mention 'proletariat'. The same problem does not seem to arise with 'workers', which appears to be more neutral in character, perhaps because, like 'labour', it has a legal status. The original connotation of working class, which still lingers with most, is that of blue-collar operatives in manufacturing industry. It may be that some sociologists now group people together more widely as working class on the basis of their relationship to the more sophisticated means of production to be found in contemporary capitalism. Thus they say there is no basic distinction between an operative and, at least, a middle manager in that neither owns or controls the firm. However, it does not follow from this that all the individuals concerned perceive themselves as belonging to exactly the same social grouping. Nor is their failure to recognise this broader definition of working class simply a defect in consciousness. Rather is it a result of other distinctions such as education, responsibility, income, job security or flexibility, and life-style.

Apart from this stratification in certain areas of employment, there is also the fact that the by now bigger and growing services sector is staffed almost entirely by white-collar workers of one grade or another. Most of them likewise do not own or direct their enterprises, but practically all of them would identify with the clerks and managers of industry rather than the operatives and for the same reasons of differences in education etc. Something that does not change this fact but makes white-collar workers increasingly open to unionisation (and hopefully in turn political involvement in progressive politics) is the tendency towards larger-scale units in the services sector. This is because of the consequential breaking down of patriarchal relations of employment.

However, what is apparent about all the persons concerned is that they are still employees and not employers. In other words, they are wage or salary earners who do not take or usually participate in decisions about the running of their employments or the use of the profits they help to produce. They therefore have no serious influence over their immediate economic environment or the wider one created for them by business as a whole and the State.

But there are some who are in the contractual position of employee, yet are such big earners and often so highly qualified and prized by the top echelons of society that they are unlikely ever to line up politically with the bulk of employees. Instead they see their interests as linked to the owners or controllers of capital. (By 'controllers' we mean the individuals in joint-stock capitalism who may not possess the entirety of a firm, but dominate it through a majority or strategic share holding.) While there is some recent historical evidence of middle-ranking managers becoming involved in radical politics, it would be hard, for example, to point to many hospital consultants in that regard. Although they may use the facilities of a trade union to some extent, they function in a strongly individualistic environment and a union is seen merely as a useful service rather than as an expression of a collective ethos or an agent for social change.

Apart from high earnings, there may be additional factors of attitude or situation that will prevent other pockets of employees from being mobilised in a progressive direction. But the hope is that these are exceptions which leave the preponderance of workers amenable to such a possibility, especially when it is presented in terms that reflect and communicate more accurately the realities and complexities of the modern world. (We exclude here, of course, those who are in reality owners or controllers of capital and are 'employees' only for legalistic and tax purposes.)

The main catchment area for progressive politics in Ireland today might therefore be seen as generally comprising the classes of low and medium-income employees. The first includes the traditional working class and lesser paid white collar workers and the second the better paid but by no means wealthy white collar person.

If it is desired to capture succinctly what all these people have in common, while at the same time not trying to ignore the distinctions among them and their self-perceptions, as well as indicate that they are the most likely to seek positive social change and be susceptible to a radical politics, then the phrase 'progressive classes' might best meet the bill. An instinctive grasp of this classification has already been made in Irish parlance with the expression 'PAYE worker'. A model for such a perspective also exists in the mixed blue/white-collar membership of the modern trade union movement. The one thing we must avoid is trying to force social life and human understanding into some rigid ideological mould and vocabulary.

As for the 'middle class', from an analytical point of view, there is really no such thing in Ireland because we do not have even a residual 'upper class' of our own in the aristocratic sense. The class of high-income employees and the owners or controllers of capital (or employer classes, if only employing themselves in the most basic instance) essentially comprise one social bloc. Though, of course, employers are stratified as well and include the small, medium and large scale as well as the break-even, well-off and rich. This high earner-employer bloc we would describe as the 'conservative classes'. By conservative is not meant trying to keep things absolutely the same, but seeking to maintain the present principles of ownership and management in society. This still allows for technical innovation and development. However, this usually takes place in fewer and fewer controlling hands, which can generate resentment not only among workers, but also the small business group, although political disaffection among the latter is something else. The conservative classes therefore include the traditional bourgeoisie (proprietors of industry etc), but we do not use this term both because of going beyond that category and because it is exotic to the general public in Ireland.

It is also recognised that some of those we have classed as medium-income employees would probably not be averse to the description of themselves as 'middle class' for the purpose of stating that they are not 'working class'. This tendency can be reinforced by an overlap of culture and life-style with the conservative classes.

As for the demarcation between the progressive classes and the conservative classes, it has often been suggested by socialists that the growth of big and multinational capital will drive the more and more hard-pressed small and especially self-employed entrepreneurs in the direction of radical politics. Naturally, if that happens, co-operation with them should not be refused and any opportunity that is seen to encourage such a process ought to be acted on. But there is no point in placing undue theoretical hopes in such a political outcome. Most small business people will never consider joining with radical forces until they are on the verge of bankruptcy. Even then, they sometimes just give up as happened with many in the face of EU membership.

The class picture in Ireland is completed by referring to the 'traditionalist' or farming classes, which might uniformly be seen as a rural kind of conservatism, the farm labourer now being on the point of extinction due to agricultural technology. But this bloc has to be distinguished from its urban analogue because the two are often in conflict, as membership of the EU has underlined, e.g. as regards food price policy. Farmers would also tend to be suspicious of capitalist expansion insofar as it is associated with pressure to move from the land. Strictly speaking, therefore, they do not represent simply a position of conserving the present system of social control, allowing as that does for an industrial-services dynamic, but also one of arresting the rural-urban balance at a certain stage of development. The farming classes are also traditionalist in another sense through being the bedrock of the religiously inspired illiberalism in Irish society.

That is not to say the urban-industrial mode of life is all good and there are not features of the rural experience, of the older as distinct from historically more recent commercialised variety, which are not worth emulating. This is so particularly in regard to naturalness of surroundings, a greater sense of community and a more stress-free style of life. However, the move towards urban-industrialism is quite ineluctable and the answer to its shortcomings is not in trying to halt the process or throw it into reverse, but rather in combining with it the best features of the old ways. The environmental movement could be an important means to this end and could result in a less sharp contrast between urban and rural.

Just as with small business, hopes have been raised in the past of an alliance between workers and small farmers. Again, any possibilities should not be overlooked or remain uncultivated. Yet, the historical experience once more has been that the objective similarity in standard of living and economic security between the two elements has not borne much if any fruit in relation to political linkage. And for much the same kind of reason, because until he or she loses the farm, inside every small farmer is a big farmer trying to get out. However, this non-climax has to be set against the backdrop of constant decline in the farming population and growth in the towns and cities, which makes it less and less of a strategic disadvantage for the Left.

It might also be said that surely the traditionalist classes should include lawyers, doctors, traders, and so on, who, like farmers, have been around since time immemorial. But there is a difference between sharing historical antiquity with farmers and being traditionalist in the sense of relating primarily to an earlier and rural type of society. Professional and commercial people are adaptable to and needed, in growing rather than diminishing numbers, in virtually any social order. And they are adept at recognising when the time has come to throw in their lot with a new dispensation.

Like all boundaries, those between classes are flexible on occasions. For instance, the conventional idea of the 'middle class' can be seen materially reasserting itself when medium and high-income employees

Social Classes & Politics

in particular articulate a common grievance about overtaxation. Moreover, some traders and professionals would tend to align themselves with the big farmers owing to reasons of business or other affiliation, but this is probably a small minority of these strata. On the other hand, among high-income employees and the self-employed, there are intellectuals and artists who will identify with the progressive cause for ideological reasons. At shop-floor level, tensions continue to arise between workers and supervisors never mind middle management, or between skilled and unskilled workers, even though they may all be in unions and sometimes the same one.

Nor should we forget that people can be of mixed class as with the small farmer who also works in the local factory or the worker who endeavours to keep a modest business going on the side. Furthermore, some skilled workers effectively maintain the tradition of the artisan through being self-employed on a very modest scale and owning their own tools, while not possessing any plant as such.

The position of the well-paid trade union leader is also interesting. Remuneration, life-style and the preference for social stability might seem to place this person in the class of high-income employees. But being employed by workers can ultimately ensure proper direction and accountability, whatever the tendency towards corporatism.[1]

There is an inevitable fluidity in all concepts of class and, especially when it comes to the individual, this includes the subjective and not always rational factor as well. It might further be said that, insofar as small business occasionally seeks curbs on big capital or small farmers want the redistribution of land, if only indirectly by means such as a land tax, they are progressive as well. That is true relatively speaking, but this does not make them progressive classes as we use the concept, because no basic challenge to the system of ownership and disposal of profit is thus posed.

Finally, reference should be made to what is emerging as a sort of underclass in Ireland - a body of people of all ages and from both blue and white collar backgrounds who are long term if not permanently unemployed. They are also partially victims of the tactic that replaces awkward workers with compliant machines. The experience, however, is probably more a blue than a white collar one, given the economic transformations occurring in modern society. It is also connected somewhat to the crime rate. We say 'underclass' because the question is of course not that of status in the productive system, but of being almost perpetually outside it.

Unemployment has a debilitating effect on the progressive classes and not merely in regard to industrial

---

[1] See Chapter Note 1, p 162.

power insofar as those on the dole cannot of course go on strike, and so on. They also tend in the main to drop out of the trade union movement thus depleting its representative strength as a lobbying and negotiating force,[2] while those at work and remaining in it naturally are primarily concerned with increasing income, and with preserving jobs rather than creating new ones. At the end of the day, unemployment is as much a political as a trade union issue. Clearly this is a sphere for recruitment by a radical party as well.

When all things are taken into account, it is felt that the relationship to the means of production of goods and services as they exist today will continue broadly to influence politico-social alignments in the community. This is so even allowing for the variations within social blocs in job security, decision-making, and financial reward. In this context, the task for the Left is the imaginative reconstruction of the classical idea (whatever about the term) of social democracy, i.e. the extension of the democratic and participative principle fully into social and economic as well as political life.

However, while what we are referring to is an area of potential support for the radical position, it is one which will take time to develop. Given levels of consciousness and the structures of Irish politics which have built up over the past eighty years since the War

---

[2] Although, the overall density of trade union membership is just 42%, with a big disparity in that between the public - 80% - and private sector - 27%. (Tom Hayes, *Trade Union Recognition & Employee Representation*, EIRI Associates, August 2000.)

of Independence, it is unlikely that a socialist party will gain the backing of a majority of the population in the near future. It should also be recalled that many individuals who are objectively in the progressive classes are not even a generation away in their mindset from a rural background. And the possibilities for socialism in Ireland, as anywhere else, have certainly not been helped by the disasters which have occurred in its name in Eastern and Central Europe. Besides, fundamental questions have been raised about what socialism should mean in the new century and they are still in the course of being answered as we have earlier considered in this book.

The initial task must be to build a people's movement based on a platform of social and economic progress rather than immediate and total change. In that way, the interests of small business and small farmers might be accommodated somewhat and lead to more acceptance of radical policies than would otherwise be the case. Although, again, there should not be too much optimism about this prospect. The specifically political objects should have a wider appeal encompassing women's rights, cultural development, environmental protection, civil liberties, administrative reform, sovereignty, and national reunification as, again, we have contemplated elsewhere in this volume.

At the same time, given the numerical strength of the progressive classes, a radical party should aim to be the guiding force of a people's movement and simultaneously be thinking and working its way towards a fully progressive society. What is envisaged is certainly not a preparedness to stand aside for other and lesser social elements to take the lead.[3]

---

[3] See Chapter Note 2, p 162, about the breakdown of the progressive classes.

5. THE INTERNATIONAL CONTEXT

From an Irish point of view, the international perspective, in extending layers of immediacy and relevance, encompasses: the European Union, the continent of Europe, the Atlantic perspective, and Third World responsibilities[1] - with varying implications for economic interest, military neutrality, political alignment, and human solidarity.

The European Union (as it is now called) was originally greeted by the Left in general and republicans in particular with deep hostility and therefore outright opposition. It was seen as a post-war regrouping of bourgeois capitalist States no one of which could any longer hope to dominate Europe, never mind the world. The only prospect was for their ruling classes henceforth to combine rather than compete and to substitute supranationalism for nationalism.[2] But supranationalism is not to be confused with internationalism, because it stopped and stops at the boundaries of capitalist Europe, even if those boundaries are now truly continental. In reality, it is an attempt at the reactionary paradox of 'euro-nationalism'. The Germans, French and Italians, mainly, and later the British, were no longer to look down on each other (at least officially), but to have a sense of place on the planet as solidaristic Europeans and pursue a collective interest thereon.

---

[1] See Chapter Note 1, p 163.
[2] See Chapter Note 2, p 163.

International Context

Although peoples in Africa and Asia, especially, might have been forgiven for seeing not so much a transcendence of aggression as a rebirth of imperialism. Had some of these same Europeans, in the first flush of democratic victory over fascism, not spent much of their energy in trying to consolidate or reconquer their colonies until they were kicked out by liberation movements? Were they then to establish an equitable relationship with them or did the term neo-colonialism have any meaning?

Even if one focuses inwardly on the new if somewhat truncated 'Europe' of the initial 'common market', was there not even there chiefly a realignment of establishments in the face of the post-war leftward drift among their electorates? The European project was presented as one of peace and progress in the part of the continent concerned, which meant, on the one hand, that a purely intra-european war was deemed no longer winnable and, on the other, that certain conditions of employment (e.g. equal pay) would have to be introduced in all States if they could not be avoided in any one - in order to eliminate unfair competition between companies across frontiers.

However, for most of the past twenty-eight years the Left failed to rally people in Ireland to any notable degree against the European Union. In 1972, only 12% of the electorate voted 'no' to membership; in 1987, 13% so voted in relation to the Single European Act; in 1992, this opposition began to rise to a small but not insignificant degree, registering at 18% to the Maastricht Treaty; the trend continued in 1998 regarding the Amsterdam Treaty, with 21% then recording a negative. Two points are probably of import here. Firstly, the 'no' vote has gone up as the issues became less purely economic and neutrality and nonalignment featured more. Secondly, the last referendum had to be conducted in the context of equal publicity being given to both sides of the argument following a court decision.

Of course, if one looks at the 'no' vote as a percentage of the poll, the situation has become more dramatic and worrying for the Government. Perceived in that way, it started at 17% in '72, jumped to 30% in '87, held at much the same with 31% in '92, and then jumped again to 38% in '98. It is not difficult to see that, at that rate of going, it could be perilously approaching 50% plus one. But the latter figures have to be assessed in the light of low polls since 1972, dropping from 70% to 44%, 57% and 55% respectively. While democratic procedures only require that the determining majority be of those who cast a ballot, it would be politically shallow and self-deceptive to ignore a measure of the real growth of hostility on the ground to the EU in terms of the percentage of the electorate voting 'no'. Naturally, we don't actually know the opinions of non-voters, but it is a sensible assumption that those antipathetic to the EU are more likely to turn out than vice versa.

In summary, 1998 marked a watershed in resistance to the EU by either means of calculation But one should not underestimate the work that still has to be done to maintain and extend an attitude which is critical of and, if necessary, prepared to reject some of the projects coming from Brussels.

It is against this backdrop that one has to weigh up contemporary tactics and strategy for the Left vis-à-vis the EU. The simple demand for immediate withdrawal is not an option. There is no reason to believe that even the fifth of the electorate who voted 'no' to Amsterdam would solidly back such a stance. Conditions are just not right either domestically or internationally for this position. The EU is still seen to be economically benefiting Ireland on balance and, while the Euro currency in particular is obviously giving rise to problems, the situation has not reached crisis proportions. Although, it should be the object of constant analysis and criticism. On the non-economic front, developments continue in foreign policy and security co-ordination which are making more and more people anxious, but again these have not become climactic. (If sons and daughters in the Defence Forces began returning in body-bags from the Balkans or wherever, the reaction might be different.) Therefore, one has to formulate a policy which takes account of these realities.

In fact, Sinn Féin's enunciation of "critical engagement" with the EU seems broadly to address the situation quite well.[3] SF has called for alliances with similarly minded democratic forces throughout the EU, both directly and through the European Parliament. It envisages campaigns with them on employment, social inclusion, democratic control, environmental protection, anti-racism, anti-militarism, and equality. Other EU institutions (e.g. Committee of the Regions) can also be utilised to promote these objectives. Particular opposition has been voiced by republicans to Economic and Monetary Union and any moves to develop a superstate.

Apart from campaigns on the foregoing issues, there is a need to address all sorts of detailed policies and EU expenditures which are constantly being decided, both on a Union-wide basis and specifically in relation to Ireland. These affect the national and daily life of the people throughout this island and there is thus a necessity to lobby and intervene as much as possible to influence the outcome of the processes involved. There is no point in pretending that they don't exist or asserting that they should be ignored. If sovereignty has been diminished, the people will not be served by refusing to protect their interests in the new context and until it may be adequately restored. Moreover, there is the requirement to promote the all-Ireland dimension and encourage EU interventions, which are

---

[3] *Sinn Féin & the European Union - A Draft Policy Discussion Paper*, Ard Chomhairle, 1999.

going to occur anyway, to be as integrative as possible in terms of the island.

Moving to the wider and truly European perspective - from the Atlantic to the Urals - the Left must assess what the transformations of the past ten years and their future implications mean for Ireland. To some extent, this leads us back to the EU insofar as several Central and East European countries are seeking membership of that body. Already, there is understandable apprehension about what new accessions may signify in respect of financial transfers and decision-making arrangements. And the Irish Government has promised to defend and advance the national interest in these regards. The task must be to ensure that it is held to this promise in the particular and concrete circumstances that arise. Beyond that, however, we have to assess what advantages there may be from an enlargement of the EU through adhesion of the kinds of States in question, assuming that may take place anyway.

Many of the prospective new member countries have profiles which are similar to Ireland's. They sprang from European empires, still have big neighbours, possess relatively small national cultures, retain comparatively big agricultural sectors, have populations concerned about military alliances, and are wary of being swamped in EU structures. In fact, mere expansion itself of the EU may well slow down, if not put paid to, ambitions to create a superstate, owing to the sheer operational magnitude and complexity resulting therefrom. Although, a fallback position of a two-tier EU, with a core of federalised richer States, is being talked about, especially in Germany, and this has to be watched carefully.[4]

But, apart from that, and in addition to transnational ideological and political networks, several smaller States themselves, East and West, may form bonds in order to influence the character and development of the EU of the 21st century so that it is not just shaped in the mould desired by euro-federalists. Indeed, the more enthusiastic of the latter can see this and are ambivalent, to say the least, about what they worry may well be over-extension. It is interesting to note that the British are pushing for new accessions and it has been commented that British Foreign Secretary "Cook's intervention is viewed with suspicion in Paris and Berlin, where it is seen as a British ploy to prevent deeper integration among the 15 existing members by accelerating the admission of new ones." [5]

A notable area of concern is that of foreign policy and security. The Single European Act of 1986 formally instituted European Political Co-operation (EPC), i.e. regarding foreign policy. The 1992 Maastricht Treaty provided for an EU Common Foreign and Security Policy (CFSP) and raised the prospect of defence being included in due course. These aspects were reinforced in the Amsterdam Treaty of 1997. Since March 1999,

---

[4] *The Guardian*, London, 13/5/00.

[5] Michael Wolsey, Deputy Editor, *Irish Independent*, 31/7/00.

NATO has also been expanding, and the overarching and so-called Partnership for Peace (PfP) straddling North America and Europe has been launched to which Ireland has recently adhered. Already, the Irish State had established a participative observer relationship with the defence alliance entitled the Western European Union (WEU). This overlaps with NATO and is recognised as the developing military wing of the EU. Currently, there are the plans for a Rapid Reaction Force (RRF), from 2003, concomitant with the EU in which an Irish contingent is to participate. Ireland may still remain aloof from a commitment to help in the defence of other EU States if attacked. But such attack is not a real and immediate danger anyway. The actual possibility is of Irish forces going into action alongside other EU contingents in some connection regarding a State or States outside the Union.

There are serious questions as to where all these initiatives may ultimately and generally lead. One thinks of a reinforcement of global north-south and trans-Ural east-west tensions. The situation for Ireland has been summed up by the security correspondent of *The Irish Times* thus: "The move towards greater EU defence involvement will coincide with the diminution of the Defence Forces' peacekeeping role in the UN, marking a major policy change on behalf of Government." [6] In

---

[6] Jim Cusack, 'Army's new Chief of staff prepared for European role', *The Irish Times*, 29/7/00.

fact, the Government is cutting UN involvement from 760 troops to 66 by May 2001.

While the Irish State has joined PfP and is committed to the RRF, it appears that it is holding firm on NATO and is still possessed of a strong neutralist tradition. Other smaller countries in Northern, Central and Eastern Europe are in or have recently joined NATO, but may still be apprehensive about positions being adopted which could exacerbate world tensions. Moreover, neutralism has deep enough roots in some other European countries - markedly Sweden, Finland, Austria and Switzerland. Irish foreign policy should be formed so as to establish appropriate linkages which will aim to put a brake on usurpation of the UN's functions by a Euro-Atlantic bloc or the assertion of a specifically euro-role in the world through what could amount to 'security adventurism'. There is a particular need to remember and reinforce the existence and purpose of the Organisation for Security and Co-operation in Europe (OSCE) which is not just a reflex of NATO or EU ambitions. It may be seen, therefore, that neutralism is far removed from isolationism. And while neutralism may have been arrived at by different ideological and geopolitical paths in various countries, that matters little. (The origins of Irish neutralism, in particular, lie in its anti-imperialist struggle and are dealt with in the next chapter.)

The next year or so will be of especial importance in terms of political critique and mobilisation, because of the new EU treaty being formulated which will have particular implications for our remaining sovereignty and, following on that, economic and social welfare, foreign policy, and military involvement. Sinn Féin and the Greens will probably be the only significant party political forces available to put up a meaningful defence of the interests of the Irish people in this situation. Although, they will likely be joined by some campaigning pressure groups.

Finally, Ireland must look beyond the northern hemisphere to the rest of the world and consider what policies it should advocate to deal with the major problems which afflict it. Clearly, we are not in a position to wield any power as such. But we ought not to underestimate our influence which is disproportionate to our size for various reasons.

First of all, Ireland is known in many countries because of missionary activity. While that may, to a certain extent, have been part of a Western proselytisation which was not always sensitive to local culture, the reputation for altruism from what was itself a colonial territory has nonetheless not gone without lasting credit. Secondly, Ireland was the first subject country in the 20th century to fight a war of liberation against empire and did not go unnoticed for that either, especially in Asia and later Africa. Thirdly, the Irish State has held to a fairly nonaligned stance at the UN and elsewhere throughout most of its existence and would still tend to be seen in the developing world as politically distinctive in Europe in a positive way, notwithstanding its commitments since membership of the EU since 1972. (Albeit the latter could change rapidly in the context of increased defence and foreign policy harmonisation in the Union.) Fourthly, Irish connections in States, which are globally or regionally powerful, such as the US and Australia, give opportunities for making an input to international policy which other countries of comparable dimension would not have. Fifthly, Irish talent in various professional, artistic and sporting spheres has contributed notably to our world profile (ironically, this may have been helped by our command of an international language in the shape of English); therefore, we tend to have access to an audience which others might not possess.

But what are the main policies that should thus be pursued? Overridingly, we should promulgate globally the policy that has been touched on in the European and Atlantic contexts, namely arrangements which lessen the likelihood of inter-state military conflict. We could start by giving good example through enshrining in our constitution a clause committing the State to military neutrality.[7] On the international plane, Ireland has taken initiatives as early as 1961 with UN Resolution 1665 on nuclear non-proliferation which is still referred

---

[7] The White Paper on foreign policy of 1996 gave commitments to not joining NATO or the WEU and to putting any proposed EU common defence policy to a referendum and adherence to these at least should be demanded as need be. (*Challenges and Opportunities Abroad*, Dept of Foreign Affairs, Dublin, 1996.)

to as 'the Irish resolution'. Moves to strengthen this position and to encourage disarmament generally as well as the outright banning of biological and chemical warfare and related research should be promoted and there are appropriate UN agencies for doing so. In particular, the horrific weapon of anti-personnel land mines should be proscribed in use and manufacture. The employment of the International Court of Justice [8] for the settlement of disputes between States could be increased and the International Criminal Court for crimes against humanity should be brought fully into effect as soon as possible.[9] The importance of the latter will also lie in being a deterrent against armed aggression and its consequences whereby those in power may ultimately be brought to account such as is happening in the case of the former Yugoslavia. However, the value of such provisions will be diminished if it is seen that they are only used against those who fall foul of the 'great powers'.

In general, the principles of democracy and human rights must be vigorously promoted and allied to development aid or economic sanction, as the case may be. UN peace-keeping missions will also remain essential and Ireland should continue both to support and par-

---

[8] Sometimes referred to as the World Court.

[9] The ICC Rome statute of July 1998 requires 60 State ratifications to bring it into force; as of July 2000, there were 14. However, ad hoc tribunals are already in existence such as for Bosnia. Unfortunately, the ICC has come too late to challenge what Britain has done in Ireland over the past thirty years.

ticipate in them, despite what has been noted earlier about current Government policy.

The UN and its agencies also require to be further strengthened and democratised. They are still too weak and over-representative of the West, and reform must take place from the Security Council downwards. Ireland could give a lead on this and garner support for change across the globe. We should not forget the precedent that, as early as the Fifties, Ireland pursued the issue of UN membership for communist China, even against the wishes of the US and others.

On the economic front, the cancellation of the foreign debt of developing countries should be urged and the roles of the International Monetary Fund and World Bank reviewed. It is both absurd and obscene that poor countries are forced to make hefty repayments at the same time as they face crippling poverty or natural disasters. But that is not enough. Aid has to be dramatically increased and be directed with certainty to solving problems rather than lining the pockets of local élites. The efforts of aid-workers are a desirable complement here and Ireland should continue to foster this dimension.

Immigration is an issue which has arisen recently in Ireland and we must play our part in welcoming both political refugees and economic migrants, without being exploited by *other European countries* which try not to take their fair share even when they have sometimes helped create the source problem. (One thinks, for example, of the foreign policy of Germany from the Balkans to Central and Eastern Europe and then its newly restrictive immigration policy.) However, the really progressive approach is to eliminate the expellant circumstance, whether that be oppression or penury. In the latter instance, the need for meaningful international transfer of finance in particular is underlined. People have a right to live and work in their own country and be with their families and friends, as the Irish appreciate only too well. After that, if they wish voluntarily to move elsewhere, that is another matter and, indeed, cultural exchange and enrichment can then be the outcome. At the same time, one must be careful of the right-wing attitude which says people should stay at home and not be allowed into Ireland or wherever, while dictators are allowed to languish and the countries concerned are simply left to their own devices. These two stances must be clearly distinguished.

In Ireland, more than many other countries, there is also an obligation to give preference in inward migration to those nationals or their descendants who were forced out of this island by poverty or persecution. Let us not forget that, while several European countries have experienced emigration, none has seen its population halved as happened here subsequent to the Great Famine.

The world environment itself must further be a matter of central concern. Policies and practices which threaten either localities or the entire planet will have to be tackled. And it is not just a question of where they occur, such as with the clearing of rain forests; it is also an issue of demands for products or resources elsewhere, including from the developed countries. The latter means that populations will have to be educated to reconsider life-styles and exercise restraint to an extent. An example with far-reaching implications is transport and the balance between private and public insofar as it both impacts on our immediate environment and calls for extraction of fuels in other countries on a scale and often in a manner which is detrimental to them as well.

A final idea that is worth considering at the international level is the establishment of a World Congress of the Irish. This could serve both the purpose of advancing Irish foreign policy to the extent that it is consensual and fulfilling a desire to be part of a global Irish community, both socially and culturally. A structure, independent of Government, could be developed to link up the many Irish societies and individuals across the planet, and an actual congress with various sub-events could be held every three years or so in Ireland. In that way, the seventy million and more Irish could have a world-wide civic forum.

6. THE ROOTS OF IRISH NEUTRALITY

Irish neutrality, in the strict meaning of the term, can only be said to date from 1922 with the establishment of the Free State and to have been reinforced with the setting up of the undeclared republic in 1937. That is because neutrality, in international law, entails the decision of a State not to become involved in an armed conflict involving other States. How far neutrality would have been practicable prior to 1938, however, and before British bases in the twenty-six counties were handed over to the Dublin Government, is doubtful. Fortunately, the test did not come until a year later. Yet, we would be very legalistic if we did not acknowledge that certain traditions in Irish history before the Treaty contributed to the adoption of a neutral stance after it.

From a progressive and democratic point of view, Ireland's international relations before 1922 were marked by three chief characteristics. The first was the revolutionary use of England's enemies, the second was her missionary activity, and the third was nationalist unwillingness to become engaged in imperial wars to the point of, at times, assisting the oppressed peoples in revolt against the British Empire.

Linkage with England's antagonists was by and large superseded by independence for the Free State. As de Valera put it during World War II: "For the first time in several centuries, Britain, whilst engaged in a continental war, has not had to reckon with a hostile Ireland."

The missions were a mixed phenomenon. On the one hand, they were culturally westernising, on the other they brought from one colonial (and later ex-colonial) territory to others humanitarian assistance by way of education, health, and technical and economic aid. In Ireland, they provided a basis for solidarity with what is now called the Third World which underpinned, in a global context, the sense of anti-imperialism.

The idea of not becoming embroiled in conflicts on behalf of England, particularly colonialist ones, provides the main thread of continuity between the historical reluctance to fight for the Empire and post-22 neutrality.

As early as the late 18th century, Wolfe Tone spelled out what remain to this day some of the most powerful arguments for neutrality. In 1790, there was a danger of war between Britain and Spain for commercial reasons. Tone quickly wrote a pamphlet, which was even more quickly suppressed, entitled *An Enquiry How Far Ireland is Bound as of Right to Embark in the Impending Contest on the Side of Great Britain* and signed it 'Hibernicus'.

The first argument he identified was that of the need to concentrate Irish energies on rebuilding the nation in order to overcome its economic limitations and. eliminate its political divisions. He declared that "the question with us is not who is wrong, and who is right? Ours are discussions of a very different nature; to foster and cherish a growing trade, to cultivate and civilise a yet unpolished people, to obliterate the impression of ancient religious feuds, to watch, with incessant and anxious care, the cradle of an infant Constitution; these are our duties, and these are indispensable." The year might as easily have been 1939.

His second main point was that England's gain would be matched by Ireland's loss: "the quarrel is *English*, the profit will be to England, and Ireland will be left to console herself for her treasure spent, and her gallant sons fallen, by the reflection that valour, like virtue, is its own reward and that she has given Great Britain one more opportunity to be ungrateful."

Thirdly, he dealt with the idea of England as a shield for Ireland (a notion which is nowadays extended to NATO): "she defends us, or perhaps does not defend us from the resentment of her, not our enemy, and so the mighty debt of gratitude accrues; and we are bound to ruin our commerce and lavish our treasure and spill our protection in a war, which she has wantonly, and unnecessarily, as to this country, plunged us into. If this be the protection of England, I for one could be well content that we were left to our own wisdom to avoid, or our own spirit to support a contest." In summary, he said: "No man has a right to run me into difficulties, that he may extricate me from them." And: "we owe no gratitude where we have received no favour."

Fourthly, Tone considered the attitude of other powers to Irish neutrality. "It may be said that Spain will not consider you as a neutral, though you may call yourselves so. But I say, if you were to address his Majesty, praying him to direct his Ministers to acquaint the Spanish Court with your absolute neutrality, do you think her so unwise a nation as to choose you rather for her enemy than her customer, and so to fling you into the scale of England, already more than a match for her?"

He foreshadowed even the concept of nonalignment by a century and a half when he stated that "we should spurn the idea of moving an humble satellite round any power, however great ... " Tone was also prepared to assure England explicitly that Irish neutrality would be in no way a danger to her. "We invade none of her rights; but we secure our own." An echo of Sinn Féin is even heard in the assertion: "everything is beneficial to Ireland that throws us on our own strength."

A few years later, in 1793, when an actual war with France broke out, Tone wrote another pamphlet reiterating the same basic position. This time, he addressed it to the Dublin artisans and signed it 'A Liberty Weaver'. In this he said: "I never could learn what good came to the poor people by a battle or a victory ... "

At the very beginning of the radical tradition, the father of Irish republicanism thus made plain that sovereignty and neutrality should go hand in hand. The federalist tendency in Irish nationalism, however, perhaps by definition, took a different line.[1]

In the Irish Parliament in 1793, Henry Grattan voted in favour of Irish support for England's war against France and, in the following year, criticised a motion even though it merely called for an investigation of the conflict. He said that "by such conduct Ireland would prove herself, instead of the best, the meanest ally of England." Therefore, "I shall this night, consistent with the vote I gave on the first day of the session in favour of the war, resist the present measure."

Although the refusal to back England in its imperial exploits has always been an understandable consequence of republicanism, it naturally tended to be given its most open expression when wars were actually threatened or in progress. Thus Irish neutrality was proclaimed in the 1790s as well as in 1914 and 1939. At the end of the 19th century, when the Boer Wars began, the separatist attitude developed into endorsement of England's antagonists because of their anti-colonialist stance.

Even in the 1840s, however, the differing perspectives of federalists and republicans were obvious in the contrast between the pronouncements of O'Connell and Young Ireland, with one saying that repeal "sought

---

[1] Federalism is used in the broad sense in this chapter to cover all those nationalist tendencies other than separatist republicanism ranging from Grattan's through Butt's position to Griffith's.

no foreign alliance" and the other that "England's difficulty is Ireland's opportunity."

Another occasion when one might have expected to come across some opposition to military support for England was during the Crimean War from 1854-56. However, Irish nationalism was in a political trough at the time: O'Connell was dead and Young Ireland had been scattered, while the IRB had yet to be founded and the Home Rule Party to take shape. Moreover, Irish territory was not directly threatened as in the earlier conflicts with Spain or France or the later ones with Germany.

In the second half of the 19th century, the dichotomy of republicanism and federalism continued with regard to foreign policy as well as other matters. However, the boundary line between the two was not always hard and fast, especially in the Parnell period. At one stage, Parnell declared that "the cause of nationality is sacred, in Asia and in Africa as in Ireland." Nonetheless, there could be no getting away from the fact that Home Rule precluded an independent or neutral position by Ireland on defence or foreign policy and this was clearly reflected in the two Home Rule Bills of Gladstone. Yet, the important distinction is that these bills were ideological fulfilment for some and merely a stepping stone for others whose aspirations would have included eventual disentanglement from England's alliances. It has been argued that Parnell was in the latter category.

By the turn of the century, new and powerful nationalist influences were at work in Ireland on both the cultural and political fronts, which later confirmed that the years of the Parnell split were not so fruitless as they had at first appeared. The GAA had expanded and Conradh na Gaeilge was launched, while various nationalist societies were at work which came together in 1900 in the first Cumann na nGaedheal, a forerunner of Sinn Féin. The Anglo-Irish literary revival was also under way.

But it was, appropriately enough, the centenary of Wolfe Tone's death which saw the gathering of forces that gave stern opposition to England's war against the Boers, in terms either of non-support for London or actual backing of its enemy. The most articulate expression of this was to be found in a new magazine edited by Arthur Griffith called the *United Irishman.*

Yet Swift and Grattan were as much heroes for Griffith as Tone and *they* certainly were not advocates of neutrality or the rights of all nations. This was one pointer to a policy which Griffith was to develop between republican anti-imperialism and federalist collaboration with empire. The Boers, he held, were like the Irish entitled to a stake in empire and should not be subordinate to the English. But the right to political independence "never was, is not, and never can be dependent on the admission of equal rights in all other peoples." Native Africans and their ilk did not feature in Griffith's critique of empire.

Perhaps the fullest revelation of his thinking on these matters was contained in his pamphlet entitled *Pitt's Policy*. It is important to stress that this was aimed primarily at unionists and may have entailed a certain propagandist exaggeration. But it links up sufficiently with the more overtly nationalist writing in *The Resurrection of Hungary* to confirm that Griffith would have been quite satisfied with, if not have preferred, an Anglo-Hibernian Empire.

Griffith believed that the Act of Union had come about because Pitt "saw clearly enough that if the Parliament of Ireland retained the independence it won in 1782, the Government of the Empire must within 30 years be equally shared by the two countries." Lord Lansdowne, he said, "clearly saw that if Ireland gave up her Parliament, she lost her rule of Empire." Griffith asserted that Pitt had two options, following the loss of the American colonies, one of which was to "substitute for the broken policy of England's Absolutism a policy of Common Empire with England and Ireland as joint rulers." But Pitt did not choose this sharing out in contrast to Count Beust in Austria who was more "farseeing" in his dealings with Hungary. "Had he [Pitt] been so, an Anglo-Hibernian Dual Monarchy would be master of the world today."

Or as Griffith also put it: "An Empire equally governed from Dublin and London was possible of expansion beyond all that the Empire had been." "The Act of Union", he protested, "was passed to prevent Ireland becoming an imperial nation." As for "the republican idea", this "found no flaming response in the heart of the Gael, essentially a believer in aristocracy." And so it went on: "Ireland was filled with vigour, hope and enthusiasm, and produced in abundance the raw material of conquest." This view was set alongside that of early German nationalism which was implicitly criticised for having "got itself mixed up with ideas of democracy and universal brotherhood."

Although Griffith's Anglo-Hibernian Empire was supposed to be, in large measure, the restoration of a state of affairs that had obtained in 1800 (or, at least, the fulfilment of a process that had been interrupted then), in reality, it was quite a new proposition and he grossly overstated the achievement of Grattan in 1782 who had won legislative, but not executive freedom.

So, before the First World War broke out, three prototypes of Irish foreign policy had been developed corresponding to: a neutral or anti-imperialist republic; an equal partner in Empire; and an autonomous adjunct of Britain. In organisational terms, these corresponded, in the main, to the Irish Republican Brotherhood, Sinn Féin and the Home Rule Party.

Before turning to the Great War and reactions to it, it is necessary to point out that Redmond's leadership embodied a more positively pro-imperialist stance than that of previous home rulers. He was one of those for whom Home Rule was an end rather than a means. In 1883, when visiting Australia, Redmond averred that it was "undesirable that two countries so closely connected geographically and socially, and having so many commercial and international ties, should be wholly separated, and that any dismemberment of the Empire, *which Ireland has had her share in building up*, should take place" (our emphasis). He literally gave flesh to these words in 1914 when he split the Irish Volunteers and urged thousands of Irishmen to their deaths in the trenches. A blood sacrifice if ever there was one.

The republicans reacted to the World War by encouraging the Irish Neutrality League. A dual monarchy still unrealised, Griffith became a member of its Committee. Other notables on it were Thomas Farren, President of the Dublin Trades Council, Countess Markiewicz, Francis Sheehy-Skeffington, and William O'Brien of the ITGWU. The President of the League was James Connolly.

Connolly represented a new strand in the neutrality tradition, which derived its inspiration from international socialism. "I know of no foreign enemy in this country except the British Government", he wrote. But Connolly was not content merely to say that war between nations was wrong, he stated how it came about and how it might be stopped. "Should the working class of Europe, rather than slaughter each other for the benefit of Kings and financiers, proceed tomorrow to erect barricades all over Europe, to break up bridges and destroy the transport service that war might be abolished, we should be perfectly justified in following such a glorious example, and contributing our aid to the final dethronement of the vulture classes that rule and rob the world." To stand aside from inter-imperialist conflict was one thing, but actually to bring about a world in which it would not happen was another - that was the mission of international socialism of which national independence was an essential ingredient.

The Irish Neutrality League held only a few meetings, which were mainly concerned with advocating an anti-recruitment campaign. However, the open, mass movement, which this might have given rise to, could not hope to survive during war-time and the organisation was soon suppressed. Both the IRB and Connolly's Irish Citizen Army fell back on secret preparations to create the Republic which could eventually proclaim its own neutrality. In the meanwhile, however, this necessitated the age-old tactic instead of alliance with England's enemies, as alluded to in the Proclamation of the Republic in 1916 by the phrase about being "supported by gallant allies in Europe."

This picture fitted in with one earlier painted by a leading insurgent, Roger Casement, in 1913 in an article entitled 'Ireland, Germany and the Next War', and published in the *Irish Review*. It was signed 'Shan Van Vocht'. "Ireland, already severed by a sea held by German warships", Casement said, "and temporarily occupied by a German army, might well be permanently and irrevocably severed from Great Britain, and with common assent erected into a neutralised, independent European State under international guarantees." Again the paradox of colonialism necessitating alliance in the first instance with its international enemy in order to achieve eventual neutrality.

The Casement strategy failed, but there was one more demonstration of Irish neutralism before the War of Independence and that was in 1918 when the British proposal for conscription was defeated by a huge show of solidarity on the part of nationalist Ireland, which even led to the withdrawal of the Home Rule Party from Westminster. The political scientist Patrick Keatinge believes that "the popular basis of Irish neutrality was enshrined in 1918".

Neutrality was next to become a major issue in the Treaty negotiations of 1921. But it had been adumbrated the previous year by de Valera with his famous Cuban proposition. While in the United States, he had said that Britain might "declare a Monroe Doctrine for the two neighbouring islands" which would limit Ireland's relations with other States. This was Casement's guaranteed neutrality with Britain the main guarantor and not Germany, and was regarded by many at the time as a watering down of sovereignty, especially as Britain was the occupying power. The concept surfaced again during the London talks and also in connection with alternatives to the Treaty. De Valera stated that the Irish "could best realise their destiny as a neutral independent state in political isolation like certain of the small States of Europe." This would entail looking after her own defence. But Britain would have none of it.

Article 6 of the Treaty stated that "the defence by sea of Great Britain and Ireland shall be undertaken by His Majesty's Imperial forces ... " And Article 7 required that: "The Government of the Irish Free State shall afford to His Majesty's Imperial Forces: ... in time of war or of strained relations with a Foreign Power such harbour and other facilities as the British Government may require for the purposes of such defence as aforesaid." Nonetheless, the Treaty was not the end of the matter for these obligations were balanced by the terms of Article 49 of the Free State constitution which stated that: "Save in the case of actual invasion, the Irish Free State (Saorstát Éireann) shall not be committed to active participation in any war without the assent of the Oireachtas."

Attitudes within the new Free State to the implications of the Treaty and the Constitution respectively on this matter were mixed. In 1927, during a debate in the Dáil, Desmond FitzGerald referred to "the point of view of maintaining our neutrality and freedom" and the veto on involvement in war under Article 49. Kevin O'Higgins, on the other hand, said that neutrality might well be "a consummation devoutly to be wished for", but there was "a certain mutuality of interests between the two countries." (Nonetheless, an official Irish defence document of a few years earlier in 1925 was couched in terms of protecting against a "violation of neutrality.") [2] Thomas Johnson of Labour grasped the practical point that "the more we disentangle our defence forces from those of Great Britain, the less risk of being involved in war we shall run." Later in 1927, when de Valera entered the Dáil, he put it bluntly that "the right of maintaining our neutrality is the proper place for this country" and suggested that the main threat of aggression came from England.

Yet, it must be said that while the *tradition* of neutrality may have been maintained to a certain extent in the Free State, its fulfilment would have been quite unrealistic in time of war because of the limitations on sovereignty. Cosgrave and de Valera approached the latter problem in different ways. The former sought, as he styled it, "to refashion the Commonwealth in closer accord with Irish interests and outlook", while the latter was out "to seek the first opportunity to unravel, and by one dramatic revolutionary stroke to sever, Irish ties with the Commonwealth." It might be claimed that Cosgrave's vision was rewarded by the Statute of Westminster in 1931, which clearly gave absolute autonomy to the Dominions. But the spirit of the Commonwealth thereafter was still in contradiction of Irish neutralism as revealed by the fact that the Irish State was the only Commonwealth State not to go to war with Germany in 1939.

---

[2] Annotated by Cosgrave: "earnest desire ... to avoid participation in any international struggle".

Roots of Irish Neutrality

The position in regard to neutrality was strengthened in 1937 with the enactment of a new Constitution deriving directly from the people (particularly Article 29[3]) and the final overthrow of the Treaty in respect of the twenty-six counties. But it was the Anglo-Irish Agreement of 1938 which ensured that the Irish State could really be neutral during World War II, when the ports at Berehaven, Cobh and Lough Swilly were handed back to the Irish Government. Churchill, of course, threw a fit at the time in the British House of Commons, but Chamberlain had not agreed to the measure without consulting his Chiefs of Staff. Keatinge's summing up of the situation is: "The ports would indeed be valuable anti-submarine bases, but it was recognised that the cost of holding or seizing them in the face of Irish hostility (involving perhaps the occupation of the whole country) would far outweigh any advantage."

One of the major features of pre-War Ireland was the State's independent foreign policy. The Free State joined the League of Nations in 1923 and became a very active participant. In 1934, the State supported the entry of the Soviet Union. The following year it backed sanctions against Italy for coercing Abyssinia. And,

---

[3] "1. Ireland affirms its devotion to the ideal of peace and friendly co-operation amongst nations founded on international justice and morality.

"2. Ireland affirms its adherence to the principle of the pacific settlement of international disputes by international arbitration or judicial determination.

"3. Ireland accepts the generally recognised principles of international law as its rule of conduct in its relations with other States."

from 1936 onwards, it observed a strict policy of non-intervention in the Spanish Civil War. These were courageous policies in the face of Western pressures and the domestic clericalist lobby which despised "atheistic Russia" and saw fascism as a necessary bulwark against communism. The main political line-up during those years may be summed up as follows. Republicans (inside and outside Fianna Fáil), by definition, were anti-Commonwealth; they favoured neutrality; and the mainstream took a reasonably progressive line generally in international affairs. Fine Gael and its predecessors were pro-Commonwealth; equivocal, to say the least, on neutrality; and sympathetic to, if not actively supportive of, fascism.

As John A Murphy has expressed it: "Neutrality in a world conflict is the ultimate exercise in national sovereignty." Or, as Keatinge opined, it was: "arguably the most dramatic and concentrated test of the state's political independence." And the abstract was at last to become concrete, but, for a while, it was not at all clear that it could. In April 1938, de Valera voiced some doubts about the prospect: "in modern war," he said, "there is not any neutrality. During the war [World War I], trade from one neutral country was stopped or interfered with by the belligerents of both sides." At the beginning of 1939, he stated: "It is possible that, despite any declarations on our part of our desire to keep out of these conflicts, if we desired and tried to carry on the trade which is essential to our economic life here, we would be regarded as a combatant, and our neutrality would not be respected."

Nonetheless, when war broke out in September 1939, all parties agreed that neutrality was the correct stance and that that was what the people wanted. Fine Gael, however, continued to have its anti-neutrality elements and, in 1942, James Dillon had to be expelled from the party on those grounds. For Labour, Norton's position was unambiguous in being reported as advocating that "as far as possible neutrality and isolation offered the best course in the event of war."

It is important to pause here and review the Irish philosophy of neutrality in 1939 after seventeen years of Statedom. Keatinge has pointed out that "neutrality had never been simply a pragmatic reaction to a dangerous world situation", although some of our rulers would have us think otherwise today. We have already identified the main justifications of neutrality from the time of Tone onwards. But new ones were added in the Twenties and Thirties of the last century. First of all, there was partition. De Valera always maintained that neutrality could never be surrendered, while this endured. Yet, he never implied that, if the problem were solved, abandonment of neutrality would be the price to pay - merely that it would be open to an all-Ireland Dáil to consider the situation. A consideration which, he clearly hoped, would lead to reaffirmation of neutrality. This would be entirely consistent with his position during the deliberations surrounding the Treaty.

Roots of Irish Neutrality

In 1940, the American representative in Dublin, David Gray, asked de Valera if he would expel the German legation and give back Berehaven to the British in return for a guarantee of Irish unity from Britain, to which de Valera replied: "No. We could never bargain with our neutrality." While this might seem a circumspect reaction to a promise, on another occasion Gray reported that he put it to de Valera that if the north "would consent to the ending of partition under suitable guarantees" would he abandon neutrality. To this, de Valera replied: "The neutrality of Ireland is not for sale." In his book on Irish neutrality, T Ryle Dwyer states that when Malcolm MacDonald from the British cabinet met de Valera, he "would not even consider abandoning neutrality until Irish unity was actually established. ... In return, the new united Irish parliament would consider whether or not to declare war on Germany and Italy."

A second reinforcement of the neutrality position came from the failure of collective security within the framework of the League of Nations. "Small states," said de Valera, "must not become the tools of any great powers" and he earnestly hoped that the League, of which he was, for a while, President, would contribute to this end. But on the eve of war, he had to admit bleakly that it was "débris". The only choice thus left Ireland was to assert and protect her own neutrality.

In September 1939, de Valera said in the Dáil that his outlook was not one of "adherence to some theoretical, abstract idea of neutrality or anything like that".

This might be used to buttress the bald, pragmatic view of the policy. However, it has already been shown to have had greater ideological strength than this. What de Valera might be taken as referring to, without contradicting the republican nationalist tradition, was that the philosophy of neutrality was grounded in Irish needs and Irish experience. In so being, it still partook of certain universal and, indeed, moral standards, but the point was that it was not a doctrinaire idea superimposed on Irish conditions; rather a principled stance deriving from them.

Two points emerged during World War II which are of lasting significance to neutralism. One was the problem of what was materially required to defend neutrality and the other was the question: how strategically important was Ireland at the end of the day?

It was Ernest Blythe who observed that "a country that will not provide for its own defence according to its capacity is not likely to have its rights protected in a spirit of pure altruism by any other country." Frank Aiken captured the idea epigrammatically when he advised that there was "no use in trying to substitute a wishbone for a backbone." As a result, the Irish State put a quarter of a million men in arms during World War II. It had no armaments industry, but persuaded the British and Americans to supply extra weapons in their own interests so that the Germans could be resisted, if need be. The whole of Ireland could have been occupied by the British and Americans if that had been considered absolutely vital. But the success of armed neutrality was that it had to be so vital before being attempted. Otherwise, the twenty-six counties might have been overrun with the same casualness as was Norway by Hitler.

Secondly, Ireland's strategic relevance depended on a number of factors. Although the ports would have been useful to the British, they could be done without. Convoys tended to come via the North Atlantic in contrast to the First World War, owing to German occupation of the French coast. And the British did have Derry and Belfast, which were crucial. The invention of radar also helped to diminish the importance of the twenty-six counties for purposes of military communications. An overriding consideration was that the Irish State was not actually located in the main theatre of war and between the contending parties. The main worry was: would the Germans attempt to invade England through Ireland? Even after Dunkirk, however, the British decided that they had better deal with that problem if and when it arose rather than endeavour to pre-empt it.

In summary, therefore, Ireland was of continuing strategic importance, and it seems ridiculous to have to say so, but it is in fact necessary because so much has been written to the contrary, both in relation to World War II and the contemporary situation. Yet that strategic importance did not make essential its occupation, which is another matter.

Indeed, an invasion of the south might have given rise to consequences outside the State. In the early years of the War there were 50,000 southerners in the British army and about 125,000 recent Irish immigrants working in British industry. Nor was the influence of Irish exiles in the Dominions to be left out of account and especially not in the United States. Furthermore, Ireland was a useful source of food supplies, which London did not want disrupted. An incursion would, therefore, have had repercussions which the threatened Allied one in Norway, upstaged by the Germans, would not have had. On the broader economic front, Britain did put pressure on the State to give up neutrality, but, apart even from food supplies, collapse of the economy in war conditions would also have had the effect of rendering the territory susceptible to German penetration.

An interesting sidelight to neutrality during World War II concerns the north. The credit is usually given to de Valera for preventing conscription there, but, in a way, he was helped along by Craigavon who said that "there is a fifth column and we require to go very carefully along the road of arming people in Northern Ireland."

Irish neutrality, of course, had to be benevolent towards the British and later the Americans and secret liaison took place among military staffs. But, all in all, that was a concession to reality which did not compromise principle or leave 700 dead in Dublin the way that German bombs did in Belfast.

Irish neutrality during World War II has been criticised on moral and political grounds. Ireland has been slovenly and tendentiously classified with other neutrals such as Portugal and Spain. Moreover, it has been claimed that it reneged in the fight against fascism.

In the first instance, it is only fair to say that many people at the time saw the Second World War as a repeat of the First, an inter-imperialist conflict, although Irish sympathy lay to a degree with Poland as another Catholic victim of colonialism. However, when the contest assumed a character of fascism versus democracy, it is generally accepted that the Irish people's sentiment lay with the latter. Surely, it was perfectly right that the part of Ireland which had been so recently freed from the depredations of imperialist subjection should concentrate on maintaining its material integrity, while politically supporting the cause of democracy. Besides, it was possible that an Irish State weakened by war would have been taken advantage of by a still predatory Britain at its close.

Outside the Dáil, the attitudes of political groups to Germany differed. Some sections of the IRA followed the precedent of Connolly and sought German aid in the struggle against partition, while expressing no sympathy with Nazism.[4] However, the circumstances were quite different from 1916; an Irish State was now in existence, which it was foolish to ignore, and whose very existence could be put in jeopardy by such tactics. O'Duffy and the remnants of the Blueshirts, on the other hand, felt an affinity not only towards Germany, but also towards the creed of fascism. If some of the IRA were mistaken, they were all culpable.

As it happened, the Irish State survived the war without violation of its neutrality and acquired a new-confidence in the process. The next major challenge it faced was the Cold War.

In 1946, de Valera, alluding to the United Nations, said: "I think we have a duty as a member of the world community to do our share in trying to bring about general conditions which will make for the maintenance of peace." But the Soviet Union vetoed Irish participation and the State had to be content with involvement in UN specialised agencies to begin with. The Soviet veto was connected with the evaluation of voting strength in the UN and Ireland was correctly assessed as, on balance, more pro-West than pro-East. Neutrality during the anti-fascist war also held against Ireland in Soviet eyes. Unfortunately, therefore, the debt of 1934 to Ireland for supporting Soviet entry to the League was not paid until 1955 when Moscow dropped its objections.

The main concern of Irish foreign policy in the immediate post-War world was partition and this over-

---

[4] For example, Frank Ryan who fought against Franco.

lapped with the neutrality question when Ireland was asked to join NATO in 1949. Seán Mac Bride's reply was direct: "Six [of Ireland's] north-eastern counties are occupied by British forces against the will of the overwhelming majority of the Irish people," therefore "any military alliance with, or commitment involving military action jointly with, the State that is responsible for the unnatural division of Ireland, which occupies a portion of our country with its armed forces, and which supports undemocratic institutions in the north-eastern corner of Ireland, would be entirely repugnant and unacceptable to the Irish people."

Some hints about the possibility of a bilateral defence pact with the United States were given by Dublin, which were in contradiction of the wider neutralist stance, but they did not mature and so were not tested in the crucible of public opinion. In the early Fifties, a pamphlet was published under the title *Neutrality and Peace*. This consisted of a number of pronouncements by a wide range of well-known personalities. In it, the policy of Irish neutrality was inextricably linked to that of world peace. A statement by William Norton of Labour was quoted in this pamphlet which dealt with the north in this context: "The Six Counties will not be sold as a condition of our participation in any international military pact."

From about the 1960s onwards, there has been an attempt to make partition the sole political objection to surrendering neutrality and then to say that NATO no more implies a compromise on this issue than membership of any other international organisation, such as the EU. In this way, it is hoped to obliterate the rest of the neutrality tradition which has been outlined. Complementary to this stratagem is promotion of the myth that Ireland has never been neutral in any sense other than abstaining from a military alliance. One point is chiefly adduced in support of this contention. For instance, during the first inter-party Government, Seán MacBride had said: "Our sympathies lie clearly with Western Europe" and during the second, Liam Cosgrave, as Foreign Minister, declared his support of the "free world". And other such statements have been made over the years by Taoisigh and Foreign Ministers.

There is little doubt that, while the options may be more hazy today, if in the past the Irish people had had to choose simply between a society based on religion and capitalism and one resting on atheism and communism, they would have opted for the former and this inevitably affected their perception of States other than their own. However, insofar as the term 'political neutrality' has been used, from time to time, by those advocating a particular worldview, it is fair to say that what has been meant is not that Ireland is or should be indifferent to the values on which global political order is based. Rather is it suggested that Ireland should take its own decisions in interpreting the values it holds and the actions which flow from them, and not merely accept the opinions and behavioural norms received from power blocs. In fact, Cosgrave articulated this aspect quite well in 1955 when he stated that Ireland should "try to maintain a position of independence, judging the various questions on which we have to adopt an attitude or cast a vote strictly on their merits."

Such an independent foreign policy, as political neutrality might otherwise be described, was evident in the Thirties at the League of Nations in examples which have already been given. It was also to be seen in the Fifties and Sixties at the United Nations, on issues such as apartheid, nuclear weapons, general disarmament, decolonisation, Algeria, and Tibet. We were not, are not and should not be ideologically neutral, although obviously there are different emphases in regard to what our ideological commitment should be exactly. Political neutrality is not ideological neutrality.

Desmond Williams has explained our position as follows: "Ireland was not a 'third world' power, nor did she belong to the nonaligned faction, though she often voted in the United Nations for motions proposed by it." He also described Ireland as playing "a third world role before its time since this was before the influx of third world countries as from 1960." There were even references in the UN around this time to an "Afro-Irish bloc". Conor Cruise O'Brien said that: "An independent 'Swedish' line is what we had hoped for." When Ireland raised the question in the UN of membership for the People's Republic of China, she did so against opposition from the United States and also incurred Cardinal Spellman's wrath, while winning no kudos at home from Fine Gael and clericalist circles. This underlines the point that, while Ireland had her values in international relations, they did not simply appeal to the lowest common denominator of domestic conservatism.

The Nonaligned Movement was formed in 1955 and it has just been noted that Ireland did not join this. A rather facile effort is made nowadays by playing with words to say that we were, therefore, never nonaligned. It may come as a surprise to some people, but non-alignment wasn't just invented in 1955, although a formal movement may only then have assumed that title. That is why Keatinge remarks of the period as early as 1922-32 that foreign "policy can be seen as directing the State away from this orientation [i.e. the British Commonwealth] to that of *nonalignment* ... " (our emphasis). And also why he speaks of "the decision to join the EEC [5] in 1961" as "the Achilles heel of nonalignment".

If 'political neutrality' may also be spoken of as an 'independent foreign policy', an 'independent foreign policy' may equally be referred to as 'individual nonalignment.' They are all basically the same thing, although capable of various modes of expression.

It has just been alluded to what was to be the watershed of Irish foreign policy in the post-war world and

---

[5] European Economic Community.

what was to break the continuity of the tradition of political neutrality stretching as it did from the days of Wolfe Tone - namely, the commitment to the EEC or what used to be called merely the Common Market. This gave the impetus to separating the issue of anti-partitionism from that of joining NATO, because it was felt by Lemass that membership of the Atlantic Alliance or at least a European defence force might be a price that would have to be paid to gain admission to the Brussels pact. In an adjournment debate in the Dáil on 8 March 1962, he dismissed the partition objection to NATO and so cancelled the policy of de Valera and MacBride. He had no opposition and only active support in all this from Fine Gael. As Keatinge points out, "the government's reluctance to criticise the major policies of the western powers" was also seen by some as linked to the application to join the EEC. In 1961, for example, Ireland lined up with them on the tactics of dealing with the Chinese question at the UN, while still holding that the admission of the People's Republic should be examined.

The only party which was definitely opposed to joining the EEC for leftist and neutralist reasons in the Sixties was the National Progressive Democratic group, whereas Labour endorsed this position in the Seventies.[6] Sinn Féin resisted on both occasions. On the cul-

---

[6] " ... the consensus of opinion at Labour's 1962 conference seemed to be that Ireland should do whatever Britain did because of export dependence on the British market" (Gallagher, ref. p 131).

tural consequences of EEC membership and connections with the broader western alliance, which is a repeated and hallowed theme, Jack McQuillan observed that this usually amounted to no more than "the clinking of glasses and long sessions at diplomatic parties."

As it turned out, Irish membership of NATO was not a precondition of gaining access to the EEC. But there are connections between the two institutions. A Eurogroup in NATO was established in 1968 and there has been the overlapping WEU since the late Forties. Furthermore, reports of the European Parliament throughout the Seventies as well as the Tindemans Report in 1976 provided a list, by no means exhaustive, of examples regarding the concern with defence. Regarding foreign policy, the first Davignon report of 1970 launched a process called European Political Cooperation which was later formalised and extended, and linked to security and defence, as dealt with in the preceding chapter.[7]

It is also quite unrealistic to think that economics and politics can be compartmentalised. If we do not go along with the Germans or the French at the United Nations on questions affecting their involvement with certain regimes, for instance, can we seriously expect them to support us when we look for a better deal on beef or more transfers in the regional policy? That is the substance of what Ireland got itself into. As a result,

---

[7] Pages 86-87.

one thing definitely changed in foreign policy after Ireland joined the EEC and that was that the national voting pattern at the United Nations came more into line with the West. Likewise, outside the UN some of our policies on specific issues were affected such as in relation to Olympic games protests about Soviet intervention in Afghanistan, and sanctions - against Iran following the taking of American hostages, and initially against Argentina over the Malvinas-Falklands conflict. Otherwise, we might have chosen alternative ways of protesting at these events.

Yet, while we do remain outside a military alliance, Irish leaders have not been unaware of the enduring value of neutrality. Garret FitzGerald of Fine Gael proclaimed in 1973, before becoming Foreign Minister, that Ireland's vote in international affairs could be "imaginative and constructive - all the more so as we are not involved in any military alliance." In 1975, another future Foreign Minister, Fianna Fáil's Michael O'Kennedy said that "our traditional neutrality in international affairs is a strong foundation on which to build our foreign policy programme." The appeal to Third World countries is obvious, although this has been put a little less attractively by Johan Galtung as the role of a fig-leaf for what is now the EU.[8] Moreover, the politicians just quoted were both in opposition at the time.

---

[8] Remark at a Dublin seminar, but see also his book (ref. p 131).

On the other hand, many Irish missionaries have become radicalised and returned development workers likewise, and they often have formed themselves into distinctive lobbies. An added source of resistance has thus grown up to the gradual abandonment of neutrality, because of its real implications for our relations with the Third World. These also embrace possible direct or indirect involvement with arms manufacture and export, including projects in Ireland. Moreover, the societies that missionaries and aid workers have encountered are ones not only of exploitation, but of revolt. They are bringing back a message both of material deprivation and moral outrage, which is touching the heart and influencing the conscience of modern Ireland. It remains to be seen whether, in the popular imagination, these messages can cast into global relief the betrayal of the humanitarian enterprise of Third World activists which often originates in the policies and practices of the developed world.

The conclusion here about Ireland and the EU is that it has largely led to the demise of political neutrality and put a question mark after military neutrality, the end of which could now be more a matter of timing rather than principle.

Finally, before summing up, we must ask ourselves - is Ireland still of strategic importance, or has this, after centuries, from the Bruce Invasion to the Aud gun-running, suddenly evaporated, as some suggest.

Authoritative voices have certainly been raised in support of this suggestion. At one stage, Nicholas Mansergh told us that "the supersession of conventional weapons by a still fortunately unconventional nuclear armament, including intercontinental ballistic missiles, has deprived Ireland, possibly for all time, of her former strategic importance." Desmond Williams wrote that our forces are "so small as to be insignificant and the technology of war rendered interest in Irish bases nugatory." This is a case of a popular notion being given academic sanction by people with little knowledge of military thinking whatever about their command of political history.

Over the years, we have endeavoured to correct this erroneous assumption by quoting from the writings and speeches of military theorists and politicians alike, both about modern war strategy and Ireland's value in particular. Fortunately, persons of greater distinction than the common run of radicals have come to a contemporary realisation of our strategic significance and herewith the last quotation from Keatinge which adequately sums up the situation: "The assumption that the state is strategically altogether irrelevant may be wishful thinking, based on the contingency of an all-out nuclear war and ignoring the preparations continually being made to deter such an eventuality. It could be argued that Ireland's peripheral situation and relative underpopulation make her attractive either as a location for missile bases or as an exemplary target. As for conventional warfare, which is still a significant element in strategic policy, Ireland could provide logistic facilities, such as deep-sea harbourage, or be the location for reserve, training or command units.

"At a more general level," he continues, "there is the question of denying any potentially hostile state the room to develop its position on Irish soil or in Irish waters. This is seen most clearly if the traditional assumption that the British Isles [sic] form a strategic entity is maintained. In 1972, for example, the British government declared, as one of its three major concerns in Northern Ireland 'that Northern Ireland should not offer a base for any external threat to the security of the United Kingdom.' The same principle applies to the whole island from the point of view of the alliance of which Britain is a major member ... ."

In this chapter, the purpose has been to show that the roots of Irish neutrality go back well beyond the foundation of the State, indeed in explicit ideological terms to the 18th century and, with perhaps even earlier resonances. Also, the endeavour has thus been to stress that the tradition is not a mere matter of government policy since 1922, but has several strands and that there is a people's tradition as much as an official one.

A philosophy has been developed over two centuries that Ireland should remain neutral because of the need:

(1) to concentrate on national reconstruction;

(2) to avoid loss without gain in foreign wars;

(3) to protect our independence against all-comers;

(4) to develop positive links with all nations;

(5) to avoid becoming a target through alliances such as with Britain or NATO;

(6) to avoid collaboration with imperialist or neo-colonialist exploitation; and

(7) to enable us to make an independent contribution to world peace and brother and sisterhood and the development of global collective security.

Here surely, is a worthy blend of the pragmatic and the principled, which covers neutrality in both its military and political aspects and is the fruit of the republican and socialist perspectives in Ireland.

The last remaining objection to or doubt about all this is not should we but can we remain neutral? Is it feasible for Ireland to provide a deterrent to invasion or can we even afford it?

The last war proved that we can build up a deterrent. The point is not that Ireland would have been occupied, sometime between 1939 and '45, if it had been crucial to the Allies or the Axis powers. Rather is it that it had to be so before such a move would have been contemplated. If Ireland had not had 250,000 men in arms and the will to resist, the State would have been overrun to eliminate the anxiety which existed about it as a potential threat. The task is at least to maintain that threshold of deterrence, if not to raise it. Maintaining it is as much a political undertaking as a military one by keeping high the spirit of freedom and the determination to resist, if need be.

Militarily, a lot could be learned from a country like Switzerland, which involves the entire population in a people's militia, although tradition here would require that to be voluntary. The Swiss appreciate that an initial conventional encounter would not be a sufficient deterrent and that it must be followed by a planned guerrilla campaign. Switzerland has even built-in destructive devices in facilities and communications which might be used by an enemy.

Of course, that country's economy is significantly better off per capita and has a greater proportionate outlay on defence than Ireland. Now that our economy has improved, however, and we are about to spend more on defence anyway in respect of materiel, the focus should not just be on an EU Rapid Reaction Force or UN peace-keeping; deterrence to invasion must continue to be on the agenda in organisation and planning and the purchase of new supplies and equipment. Apart from that, an intelligent strategy of appropriate physical and tactical preparations should be adopted to impede penetration of the country by an enemy.

Where is the threat, some might say? Of course, none is evident at the moment. But it was there in 1922 when the British might have invaded if the civil war had gone the 'wrong' way. It was there in 1939-45 from both Germany and Britain (and the US). Nor was the potential absent from the Fifties to the early Eighties, if the

Roots of Irish Neutrality

Cold War had become suddenly hot - and there was more than one occasion when it could have.[9] Only the historically amnesiac or naïve would think that there could never come another time in which the nation faced such an external danger. When one casts an eye across the globe, it is not that removed from tensions which could still explode right into the heart of Europe with repercussions which are unforeseeable today. Let us trust that it doesn't happen, but also let us, like every other nation, be somewhat ready in case it does.

We finish here with one more saying of the man whom we first referred to in this chapter, Wolfe Tone, which could be the simple motto for us even today: "Peace with all the world ... is our object and our interest."

REFERENCES

Seán Cronin & Richard Roche (eds), *Freedom the Wolfe Tone Way*, Anvil, 1973.
D O Madden (ed), *Grattan's Speeches*, (2nd ed) James Duffy, n.d.
F S L Lyons, *Ireland Since the Famine*, Fontana, 1973.
John A Murphy, *Ireland in the Twentieth Century*, Gill & Macmillan, 1975.
Arthur Griffith, *Resurrection of Hungary*, (3rd ed incl appendix *Pitt's Polcy*), Whelan & Son, 1918.
C Desmond Greaves, *The Life and Times of James Connolly*, Lawrence & Wishart, 1972.
T P O'Neill & the Earl of Longford, *Éamon de Valera*, Arrow, 1970.
T Ryle Dwyer, *Irish Neutrality and the USA*, Gill & Macmillan, 1977.
Kevin B Nowlan & T Desmond Williams, *Ireland in the War Years and After 1939-51*, Gill & Macmillan, 1969.

---

[9] The Berlin Wall crisis, the invasions of Hungary and then Czechoslovakia, the Afghan crisis, the collapse of communism in central Europe.

Roots of Irish Neutrality

Conor Cruise O'Brien, *To Katanga and Back*, Four Square, 1965.
J J Lee (ed), *Ireland 1945-70*, Gill & Macmillan, 1979.
Kevin Rafter, *The Clann - The Story of Clann na Poblachta*, Mercier, 1996.
Michael Gallagher, *The Irish Labour Party in Transition 1957-82*, Gill & Macmillan, 1982.
Patrick Keatinge, *The Formulation of Irish Foreign Policy*, IPA, 1973.
Patrick Keatinge, *A Place Among the Nations - Issues of Irish Foreign Policy*, IPA, 1978.
Johan Galtung, *The European Community - A Superpower in the Making*, George Allen & Unwin, 1973.
Eunan O'Halpin, *Defending Ireland - The Irish State and its Enemies since 1922*, Oxford University Press, 1999.

7. MODERN REPUBLICANISM

Hostile critics of republicanism like to depict it as caught in a time warp whose chief boundaries are the Easter Rising of 1916 and the end of the second Dáil in 1922. It is portrayed as musing about Gaelic myth and rural idyll, subscribing to a non-existent government of *the* republic, and attached to a Catholicism which regularly denounces it. Such critics, who find it difficult to engage with modern republicanism, thus concentrate on knocking down their own anachronistic aunt Sally.

Modern republicans, however, do not base their position merely on what took place in 1916 or the general election of 1918, although those events are still germane; that is insofar as they asserted a principle - the right of the people of Ireland to *untrammelled* self-determination - which is contravened to this day through the incorporation of the six counties in the UK. They view the twenty-six county State as thus short of satisfying Irish national aspirations, but perceive its value as a popularly endorsed and vital bridgehead towards a sovereign Ireland. They wish to see a new accommodation among Irish men and women in a situation of unity, but recognise that this does not infer cultural homogeneity or administrative centralism. They do not expect Irish to be restored in the foreseeable future as the main language of the nation, but treasure its heritage and seek genuinely (in contrast to other parties) to promote bilingualism as far as possible. They do not envisage an Ireland of contemporised *tuatha*,[1] but strive to promote an enabled collective self-help [2] that eventuates in social justice and local empowerment for all; self-rule and self-respect go together at all levels. They regard these aims as necessitating the construction of a progressive alliance which is primarily, but not exclusively, rooted among wage and salary earners, forming as they do the overwhelming majority in the Ireland of the new century. But this should not be misunderstood as excluding the regional or inferring an anti-rural outlook. Moreover, they are decidedly not a Catholic party or in thrall to the Catholic church as their policies, such as on abortion, amply demonstrate.[3] Catholicity for republicans is purely a private matter.

Republicanism is therefore essentially about the people, as the very origin and political core of the word indicates - *res publica* or public good. This should entail a concern for their welfare in all its material and intellectual dimensions. The people with whom republicans deal are not just consumers or producers, or employees or employers. They are persons located in a specific national context with a potential for all-round fulfilment who ought to be provided with the means to real-

---

[1] The communal groupings at the heart of Gaelic society.

[2] This could be the modern political translation of Sinn Féin (lit. *ourselves* or self-reliance).

[3] Abortion is to be regarded as permissible where a woman's life or mental health is at risk or in grave danger, and in cases of rape or sexual abuse according to *Women in Ireland*, SF, March 1999. The same document also calls for the decriminalisation of prostitution.

ise that end. Such fulfilment requires giving scope to civic virtue, countering cynicism and extirpating political corruption. It necessitates a recognition of both cultural value and individual worth. Furthermore, 'the people' genuinely denotes the entire population and not some propertied or moneyed subset thereof. The people are thus to be regarded as citizens with rights and not just as subjects with obligations; they are equal, not subordinate.[4]

The one thing that has not changed in republicanism is esteem of Irishness. It does not suffer from neo-colonial insecurity or 'euro-indifference' to nationality. It acknowledges ethnicity in its positive aspects while, with a characteristically democratic spirit, firmly rejecting chauvinism or racism.[5] It comprehends that the nation of the early 21st century cannot be the same as when nationalism first emerged upon the modern historical scene, but discerns that 'post-nationalism' has already been falsified by history. The global is truly with us, but so also is the 'glocal'.[6] Republicans advocate overcoming individual alienation through appreciating national community; this is also the alternative to a slide towards cosmopolitan anomie. At the same time, it in no way cuts across human solidarity. The task is to help create and participate in a world democratic order

---

[4] See Chapter Note 1 on 'social republicanism', p 164.

[5] See Chapter Note 2, p 164.

[6] See Chapter Note 3, p 165.

that combines interdependence and national distinctiveness.

Sinn Féin, which is the main embodiment of republicanism today, is the only notable force in all-Ireland politics that also harbours a healthy scepticism about the European Union and its military ambitions as well as wider developments in NATO and the so-called Partnership for Peace.[7] It is the only authentically national party in the Assembly and the Dáil, through its very presence in both legislatures and continuing to reject the principle of partitionism. It has called for right of participation by northern MPs in the Dáil and northern votes in Presidential elections and relevant constitutional referenda. It is thus unique as a party on the island of Ireland in reflecting a thirty-two county mentality and practice. It could also eventually be the only party sitting on both sides of the North-South Ministerial Council. Republicans further maintain a critique of 'social partnership' and the effect on the less well-off in the community.

Their realistic nationalism, mature Irishness and social progressiveness set them apart from the opportunistic populism of Fianna Fáil, the shapeless conservatism of Fine Gael, and the non-nationalist corporatism of Labour - as well as the occasional junior partners of

---

[7] The Greens share this circumspection, but have no significant presence in the north.

[8] The LP-DL merger document spoke even more trendily of "post-nationalist", while Ruairí Quinn has openly confessed to being "corporatist", *Irish Times* 30/4/99.

Modern Republicanism

some of those parties. Furthermore, they are, therefore, also distinguished from the residuum of the anti-republican caricature which cannot look beyond the second Dáil. To put it in another fashion, for those whose position is not right-wing, not tokenistically Irish, and not economically reductionist, republicanism offers political expression.

And republicanism should not be counterposed to nationalism in the Irish sense - the distinction is that all republicans are nationalist, but not all nationalists have been republican. In other words, republicans believe in the rights of the Irish nation, but nationalists have not always agreed that these should assume a republican form. Redmond accepted the empire and Cosgrave the Commonwealth; and their political reincarnations exist to this day.[9]

Despite all this, some middle-class nationalists and others believe that what has transpired in the past twenty-five years is the co-option of republicanism, its constitutionalisation, its absorption in the broader establishment, indeed its defeat - even if this had to be ironically accompanied by giving republicans a place in power at the same time as allegedly neutralising their radicalism.

Such smug observers fail to understand that republicanism has abandoned none of its radicalism or objectives. What has happened is that a greater grasp of re-

---

[9] See also Chapter Note 4, p 165.

alities has been acquired and methods have been developed accordingly. There has been an internal critique which has led to self-defeating nonsense being jettisoned such as parliamentary abstentionism in Ireland and not recognising the institutions of the Irish State. Tactics and principles have at last been distinguished. The different elements of unionism and Protestantism and their interactions with the British have been identified and evaluated. In other words, orange supremacism and reformation liberalism have been disentangled as have their respective historical linkages with colonialism and metropolitan democratisation.[10] The need for transition in relation to the ultimate goal has been appreciated.

Moreover, republicanism is still a movement, not just a party. Its locus is not parliament but the people. That is not to say that it does not accept the extent to which parliaments reflect the will of the people, but that, in contrast to other political organisations, its Deputies do not control the movement; it controls them. And, consistent with that, republicanism has lost none of its sense that politics, while it cannot and should not be ignored in the Dáil or Assembly, is not restricted thereto. Politics must continue to be about direct involvement of the people.

Some on the Left, who might concede what has just been outlined, will say that what has transpired is pro-

---

[10] For more about this, see 'Unionism and Britishness' in *op cit* (36), '96, p 44.

gress beyond petty-bourgeois romanticism and as a consequence of a shifting class base, not least insofar as republicanism today is mainly an urban phenomenon compared to its strongly rural nature earlier last century. Another manner of expressing this is to state that politics is replacing militarism. And there have been factors of élitism and illusion which have had to be overcome.

Yet, while there is some truth in such judgements, it is not that simple. The changes have come out of a process of struggle which is the greatest educator of all. If one is failing to achieve one's objectives by certain means, then one must adapt or fade away. It could also be said that the secular, democratic and anti-imperialist kernel was always there and eventually won fully through. Moreover, as we have already argued, there is the gap in Irish politics to be filled to the left of Labour and beyond the verbal republicanism of Fianna Fáil which has become increasingly evident.

Republicanism has adapted. But it has not thus been emasculated. To think it has is the mistaken interpretation of those who preen themselves with the thought that they were always correct and that republicans have finally come to see the error of their ways. Adaptation is not emasculation and present politics is not a denial of previous resistance.

But republicanism cannot expect to move forward without accepting that some terrible things have happened and indefensible risks have occurred in its name, particularly in recent decades. This must be admitted in the face of the people and among republicans themselves in order to preserve credibility and integrity. For those who were not in the front line, militarily or politically, it is easy to say that. War is a horrible thing and gives rise to frightful deeds, even when it is a reaction to injustice and oppression. That is true the world over. Passions are enflamed and understandable rebellion can nonetheless become ruthless or reckless in its own right. Yet, the fact that a population suffers harassment cannot vindicate any and all responsive actions. There must be a constant *internal* struggle to ensure that repression does not undermine one's own moral standards. That this has to be put on the record seems evident in Gerry Adams' acknowledgement on more than one occasion of the hurt thus caused.

At the same time, one also cannot forget that those who jumped most on the bandwagon of condemnation rarely reserved as much bile for the State perpetrators of injustice as for the recipients of it.[11] Furthermore, there are those who resignedly accept excesses as unfortunate and inevitable when committed by governments in official wars, but plead no such mitigation when an oppressed people is in revolt.

In its progressive nationalism, republicanism is also in tune with the dawn of the new millennium. Those

---

[11] Let us recall the Falls curfew and that the European Commission of Human Rights found the British guilty of torture in the north and the European Court found them culpable of inhuman and degrading treatment.

who thought that the close of this century would be marked by the death of the nation are both disappointed and discredited. What many of us argued when it was neither welcome in the media nor academically respectable is now being affirmed and analysed - that the nation will endure, and ought to, although with certain transformations in the context of globalisation.

At the same time, republicans have their feet firmly planted on the ground and know, for all that has been said above, that they are not going to be propelled in meteoric fashion to political hegemony of the Irish nation. But the possibility is there to become strong enough throughout Ireland so as to make a significant intervention generally on the island and just as has happened in the six counties.

While the chief organisational expression of republicanism in Ireland today is undoubtedly Sinn Féin, that ideological outlook is not confined to that party. Whatever about their leaderships, republicans are also to be found in Fianna Fáil and Labour and many will remain there for reasons of tradition or because that is where they can have most impact. Republicans are also active in non-party pressure groups or may be in no organisation at all. Indeed, they may be included among non-voters, owing to the lack of appeal of the major Dáil parties. The strengthening of Sinn Féin will be important, but the mobilisation of republicans cannot be measured just in that fashion. The growth of that party will have a catalyst effect on republicans elsewhere and there should then be dynamic interaction with them. The fruits of such a development will be gauged, among other things, by the changing positions and policies of other parties. Moreover, republicans should reach out to all democrats where there is agreement on some if not all issues.

Republicans must also be acutely conscious of the extent of transformation being demanded of unionists. While there will always be unreconstructible supremacists among them, the signs are that a new, realistic and not altogether unrepentant unionism is emerging. Republicans, and nationalists generally, should credit the effort thus involved in striving to break with the past of colonial fascism and accept democracy and equality. While we believe that the latter principles will help advance the cause of a united Ireland, unionists should be free to advocate, by all legitimate and non-coercive means, the maintenance of the union with Britain. In the process of dialogue, some may change their minds in changing circumstances. Otherwise, broader, progressive forces in these islands may simply overtake them. But, at all times, there should be human respect, if not political agreement, and civic reconciliation, if not ideological convergence.

A question which is now increasingly coming to the fore is whether Sinn Féin should contemplate coalition in the south as well as power-sharing in the north. It is important to approach this without succumbing to the dogmatism and fetishism that once bedevilled the subject in the Labour Party. Or else, one will be in danger of creating a new confusion between tactic and principle when one has just got over that on abstentionism.

A decision on coalition should be determined by a programme for government and judgement as to the longer term impact on party development. If concessions on the right policies can be secured and implemented, and it is perceived that Sinn Féin is responsible for them, then there is no reason why coalition should not be entered into and why it should not benefit the party. But public relations will be as important here as political negotiations. In other words, Sinn Féin must not only be successful, but be seen to be so and not hesitate to constantly advertise its achievements as distinct from just a government's.

There is a myth that participation by a small party in government necessarily leads to its eclipse and decline. The evidence which is currently most frequently adduced to that end is the advance of the Labour Party in 1992 and its reverse five years later. However, the historical evidence does not bear out that interpretation. After going into coalition with Fianna Fáil, Labour's standing in opinion polls remained high. It only began to go down in the wake of croneyism in political appointments and the adoption of unpopular measures such as the amnesty benefiting big tax evaders. The myth endures because of tendentious pundits in the media who are either irrationally anti-coalition or just rabidly anti-Fianna Fáil. Earlier such experiences of small parties were also more complex than is made out by the inquisitors of coalition heresy.

On the other hand, there will be times when the deal on coalition or share-out of posts is not good enough and power at all costs must be avoided. When one goes into government with a party which people voted against without gaining significant ministries or securing modification of the policies espoused by it, then in time one will indeed be punished. Nonetheless, there may be occasions when policies and portfolios are *not* the determining consideration. If a party, such as Fianna Fáil, comes to be so discredited because of low standards or arrogant disregard for the people,[12] it may not be an acceptable coalition partner whatever the concessions it offers and until it purges itself of the offending elements. Trustworthiness and probity are prerequisites for any coalition. But that is still a different matter from dogmatic anti-coalitionism.

Overall and on careful analysis, there is reason to believe that many people are more policy driven than party loyal or hostile. This is also probably so because the electorate is generally astute enough to understand the consequences of a system of voting and constituency boundaries which now makes coalition of one sort or another almost unavoidable. That is if there is not to be a minority single party administration, which has been avoided since the late Eighties for reasons of sta-

---

[12] Take, for example, the decision to betray its manifesto pledge of a referendum on PfP.

bility. In this realisation, they are well ahead of some media cognoscenti and purist ideologues. The party in modern Ireland which will never go into coalition may never go into government; if it is a small party, it certainly never will.

There is furthermore often an implied and ironic élitism in the case of some anti-coalitionists. That is, when the possible, tactical advances that could be made on policies and actions through coalescence are in fact acknowledged by them, but they maintain that the 'ordinary' people cannot see this and will thus desert a left-wing party in such a circumstance. In this way, they reveal an underlying lack of faith in democracy and evince an arrogance whose result is irrelevance.

In summation, republicanism does not hesitate to be visionary in a way which is youthful and committed, nationalist and internationalist, idealistic and practical. There is a psychology and an ethics to it as well as a politics and an economics. Republicans want people to be suffused with a pride in their country and a sense of injustice at deprivation. They want them energetically and devotedly to challenge and change things. Republicans want people both to cherish their roots and look outwards towards the best example that fellow humanity has to offer. They want them to be both hard-headed realists and unashamed dreamers so as to meaningfully engage the present and imaginatively construct the future. Republicanism has no place for the weary, the self-seeking, the negative, the despondent. It characterises the new Ireland.

NOTES TO CHAPTERS

2. THE GOOD FRIDAY DOCUMENT

1. UNIONISTS & SELF-DETERMINATION

Professor Joe Lee of UCC argues that, in principle, unionists should not be ruled against their will any more than northern nationalists. However, writing in *The Sunday Tribune*, on 6 September 1998, he said: "By denying in principle the right of [northern] nationalists to self-determination, on the calculation that the numbers game will always play in their favour, unionists have deprived themselves of any right to the same claim." In other words, by unionists holding that northern nationalists should be kept forcibly in the UK as long as there are enough unionists to ensure a six-county majority for that, they have undermined any objection they might have to incorporation in a united Ireland once there is a six-county majority for that.

The Good Friday Document and the Northern Ireland Act 1998 in fact embody the latter position. That is why unionists tabled an (unsuccessful) amendment to the Act to try to make the majority henceforth in effect one of unionists rather than of voters. As Peter Robinson summed it up: "Why should the majority outlined in the Bill to take Northern Ireland out of the United Kingdom be a majority of a simple variety?" With the nationalist proportion of the population fast approaching 50% plus one, why indeed? [1]

2. IMPLEMENTATION & ACCEPTANCE OF GOOD FRIDAY DOCUMENT

In its statement on 16/11/99 to help resolve the decommissioning impasse, Sinn Féin called for "implementation of the Good Friday agreement in all its aspects." This formulation or a variation of it has been used before and since on several occasions. However, full implementation is not the same as total acceptance. The objectionable *principle* of northern majority consent does not entail any implementation. By definition, implementation means *action*, i.e. in current terms, operating the Executive, North-South Ministerial Council etc. For republicans, implementation would only arise in relation to northern majority consent, albeit still not a principle, insofar as it may come to exist in *fact* and require a plebiscite to demon-

---

[1] *Hansard (House of Commons)*, 22/7/98.

strate that. Speculation about "contrary indications" to this position arise from a failure to make this distinction.[2]

3. 'PRO-UNION CATHOLICS'

(Letter from D Ó Ceallaigh in *The Irish Times*, 29 July 1997.)

In his column on 26 July, Garret FitzGerald returns to two favourite themes of his, namely the future demographics of religious denomination in the six counties and the extent to which Catholics there may be construed as being in favour of the Union. While the first inevitably involves the speculative, the second concerns current and historical data some of which he is economical with and others of which he ignores.

First of all, he refers to an opinion poll of thirty years ago wherein "only 30 per cent of Catholics then saw an independent united Ireland as their preferred option." However, he does not mention that respondents were given another option, i.e. a 'united Ireland linked to Britain.' As has been rightly commented, the latter is somewhat unclear, but it could include what is nowadays being referred to as an 'east-west dimension', which is not incompatible with the fundamentals of Irish nationalism. In 1967, 50% of Catholics opted for this; in other words a total of 80% were for a united Ireland in a form which is inconsistent with continuance of the present Union.

He then goes on to refer to the late John Whyte's book *Interpreting Northern Ireland* and its indication that "in only one poll out of 25 conducted between 1973 and 1989 did as many as half of northern Catholics state a united Ireland as their preferred option." However, Professor Whyte also pointed out that there is a distinction between immediate hopes and long-term objectives (which may reflect fatalism as much as ideology) and states: "In 1974 77 per cent and in 1982 82 per cent of Catholics favoured a united Ireland sometime in the future."

A distinction that is further often glossed over is that, in some polls, only a minority of Catholics insist on what would today be termed a unitary Irish republic, but an overwhelming majority opt for

---

[2] Todd. 'Nationalism, Republicanism and the Good Friday Agreement', in Ruane, Joseph & Todd, Jennifer, eds, *After the Good Friday Agreement*, UCD Press, 1999.

Notes to Chapters

arrangements from independence through joint authority to a confederation all of which entail dismantling the present Union.

In any event, and dealing lastly in the matter of polls with the recent Social Attitudes Surveys mentioned by Garret FitzGerald and the around 35% Catholic pro-Union attitude cited in these, common sense would tell us that, while all opinion polls should be subject to scepticism, in the fraught conditions of the north, they are especially something to be wary of. As Professor Whyte put it in low-key fashion: "There is a reason to believe that in Northern Ireland people tend to sound more moderate than they really feel when replying to interviewers."

But, above and beyond all this, one has to decide if one is a pollocrat or a democrat. The data from the last census in Northern Ireland would suggest that in the voting age cohorts, between 36% and 39% at least are Catholic or from that background, depending on certain assumptions of analysis. And that is the level of support that nationalist parties (SDLP & SF) get in elections [since exceeded]. If there were so many pro-Union Catholics, one would at least expect them to vote for the Alliance Party and so diminish the overall nationalist vote. Garret FitzGerald has no regard to these data at all.

In conclusion, the idea of a significant number of Catholic unionists seems at times like a chimera entertained by northern unionists, and some southern liberals not renowned for their nationalism, either to console themselves or mislead others.

[Subsequent figures simply confirm the above points.]

4. NATIONALISTS & A PLEBISCITE ON UNITY

Looking at the last Westminster election in the north (1997), with a higher poll than for the Assembly, a total of 317,735 votes was cast for explicitly nationalist parties (i.e. SDLP & SF) and a total of 399,306 for explicitly unionist ones; the latter figure goes up to 462,278, if the Alliance Party is included; 10,765 votes went to other parties whose supporters' position on the national question could not be determined (including Workers Party voters at 2,766, as distinct from the leadership). The definite nationalist vote measured against all of the rest was therefore 77,655 short of 50%+1. However, if one gave half of the 'other' vote (5,383) and a quarter of the Alliance vote (15,743) to the national position, one gets the figure of 56,529. At the other end of the spectrum, if a breakdown of 1991 census figures according to voting age cohorts is used taking Catholic and non-Catholic background as a guide to nationalist and unionist position respectively, the former would be about 116,218 short of a majority.

In presenting points at meetings about nationalist fertility and unionist emigration and how these factors might in time affect a plebiscite, some pseudo-liberal and ultra-leftist criticism has been encountered, virtually to the effect that one should not refer to never mind assess these phenomena. However, an intelligent and scientific approach requires that one weighs up the social context in which one operates and how it is likely to affect politics, including winning in a poll. That is not the same as urging reproduction bonuses for nationalists or penalties for unionists for remaining in Ireland. The fertility and migratory points only become reactionary if they were employed in such a fashion or as substitutes for political struggle. Of course, even in a merely sociological way, reference to them may discommode unionists, but that is just unfortunate.

5. DIMINISHED SOVEREIGNTY & CONTRADICTIONS?

It may be said that the point about the Good Friday arrangements further diminishing the Act of Union is in fact contradicted by two statements in the Document. The first is in the Part on Strand One (i.e. the six counties) and Paragraph 33, wherein there is a reference to: "The Westminster Parliament (whose power to make legislation for Northern Ireland would remain unaffected) etc." (This is also reflected in Section 5[6] of the Northern Ireland Act 1998.) The second statement, in the Part on the Intergovernmental Conference and Paragraph 4, is: "There will be no derogation from the sovereignty of either Government."

But, if one makes the assumption of consistency rather than contradiction within the Document, these statements have to be: viewed in their immediate context; considered in regard to the precise language used in different locations; and construed alongside what has been agreed in relation to the North-South Ministerial Council (NSMC).

Regarding the first quotation about the overriding authority of Westminster, this occurs in the Paragraphs of the Document dealing with the Assembly. It does not occur where the NSMC is provided for. Moreover, the "legislation" is specified as concerning "non-devolved issues" and "international obligations", i.e. non-NSMC matters.

As for the second quotation about unaltered sovereignty, as this occurs in the Paragraphs about the Intergovernmental Conference, it can again be interpreted as relating to areas outside the scope of the NSMC with "non-devolved Northern Ireland matters" once more being highlighted. Moreover, at the end of Paragraph 9 in this Part, there is the additional statement that "The Conference [comprised principally of the two sovereign governments] ... will have no power to override the democratic arrangements set up by this agreement", which can be taken as further underpinning the role of the NSMC. It is also important that the Conference (in reality, largely the continuance of the Anglo-Irish Agreement) is there to complement the NSMC and give the Irish Government (to which appropriate representations can be made by northern interests) an input on non-devolved matters.

Besides, if this relative approach of interpretation is not adopted and a more absolutist one adhered to, one could say that the mention of "no derogation from the sovereignty of either Government" also refers to the claim of the Oireachtas to rightful jurisdiction over the six counties in a situation where Articles 2 and 3 had not yet been amended!

Looking at the Part on Constitutional Issues, at (v) there is also a reference to "the sovereign government with jurisdiction there [NI]". But here, and in connection with the other points we are making, constitutions still refer to the "sovereign" where the term was originally introduced in an absolutist legal sense and modern law reinterprets this in a more confined way, e.g. in respect of partial cession of sovereignty to the EU or whatever (such as the NSMC). Article 5 of the Irish Constitution ("Ireland is a sovereign, independent, democratic State.") was an absolutist statement in 1937, but is also regarded as a relative one since entry to the EU.

6. SECESSION OF NORTH FROM UK NOT AUTOMATIC

Concern has been voiced at the deficiencies in changes in British constitutional law in the Northern Ireland Act 1998. Firstly, secession is not automatic after a positive result for unity in a six county poll, because "proposals" to that effect must be put to and approved by Westminster. Secondly, the Secretary of State decides on when a poll shall be held in the first place. Thirdly, seven years must elapse between any two polls. These criticisms are fair enough, but do not vitiate the point that, while the Section in question could have been better in these regards, it is still an advance on the position obtaining heretofore. However, even if the Section were better, there is still the overriding difficulty in British law that Parliament is supreme and can renege on its anterior commitments. The task in either situation would be to make such an outcome politically impossible.

It should further be observed, although it is probably not of great legal import, that, in contrast to 1973, the reference to "Northern Ireland" being part of "Her Majesty's dominions", as distinct from the "United Kingdom", is not in the Northern Ireland Act 1998; but that may be just a political change to make the text more palatable to nationalists.

7. THE NEW ARTICLES 2 & 3

The new Article 2 removes the definition of the national territory. However, it continues to refer to the "island of Ireland" and recognises the "entitlement and birthright" of every person born therein to be "part of the Irish nation". This at least moves towards a definition of the Irish nation which was not previously in the Constitution. However, strictly speaking, being part of a nation is not a right; it is a fact from which rights flow. Being "part of a nation" may not mean much here legally, except insofar as the point about citizenship addressed below arises.

This redraft is compatible with the idea elsewhere identified of 'nationism' as distinct from nationalism.[3] The first demands cultural and other appropriate rights, but does not require, as does the second, that one be located in a State coterminous with the nation to the extent that that is possible. (That is to say, one could not have a State coterminous with an Irish nation defined as encompassing Irish-America, and so on, but one could have an Irish nation-state on the island of Ireland whether or not the boundaries would be those of the island.) 'Nationism' has been promoted in Ireland by, among others, Fergus Finlay, former advisor to the Labour Party, and articulated by Dick Spring while Leader thereof. It suits the economistic inclination of that party to sweep the national question under the carpet. In fact, it is redolent of Austro-Marxism's approach to nationality in the Hapsburg Empire.

On the particular question of citizenship, the second sentence in the new Article 2 initially seems curious: "That [i.e. to be part of the Irish nation] is also the entitlement of all persons *otherwise* qualified *in accordance with law* to be *citizens of Ireland*" (emphasis added). The mention of "*otherwise* qualified" seems to imply that persons referred to in the first sentence (born in Ireland) are auto-

---

[3] *Op cit (36) '96*, p 44 (pp 143-144 therein).

matically qualified for Irish citizenship [4] (although they might still have to formally claim it); but then why is that not explicitly stated (i.e., entitled 'to be part of the Irish nation *and to Irish citizenship.*')? In other words, if the latter is in reality so, the second sentence then refers only to persons not born in Ireland being part of the nation by virtue of citizenship granted by statute. (If the first sentence had in fact been more explicit, a drafting consequence is that the initial word "That" in the second would have had to be substituted for as in the square brackets above.)

The third and last sentence reads: "Furthermore, the Irish nation cherishes its special affinity with people of Irish ancestry living abroad who share its cultural identity and heritage." This is worthy enough, but doesn't mean much in law, although it infers, taken along with the preceding sentences, that, for example, Irish-Americans who are not Irish citizens are not, by way of constitutional entitlement, *part of the nation*.

There could be something of a mixture in the redraft of Article 2 of the *legal* concepts of *nationality* and *citizenship*, on the one hand, and the *political* concept of the *nation*, on the other. Citizenship as a legal idea is quite clear: it confers a civil (or civic) status vis-à-vis the State, but does not of itself politically signify that one is a member of a particular nation, however defined. The point is most striking in a multi-national State; for example, in the USSR, Soviet citizenship was shared by all, but many nations were involved.

However, "nationality" is also used in law sometimes as a synonym for "citizenship", still without seeking to imply membership of a nation as a socio-cultural unit where that happens to be the main basis of the State. This usage is evident in the title of the Nationality and Citizenship Act 1956. For this very reason, such a legal use of "nationality" has been effectively admitted by the Review Group on the Constitution to be confusing to an extent.[5] (The same point arises elsewhere with the legal use of the term "national[s]".)

Part of the consequence of the mixture is that the constitution now cuts across the foregoing points politically by in effect saying that one can become part of the *nation* as a socio-cultural unit sim-

---

[4] Thereby elevating from statute to the constitution *ius soli* (law of soil) citizenship (i.e. automatic by place of birth). The alternative is *ius sanguinis* (law of blood) citizenship (i.e. automatic by descent).

[5] *Report of the Constitution Review Group*, Stationery Office, 1996.

ply by virtue of *citizenship*. However, again, this aspect is unlikely to have any legal relevance.[6]

In summary, while the new Article 2 is at least an assertion in political terms of an entitlement to be part of the *nation* for those born in the island, it neither politically nor legally (and especially in the light of the new Article 3 about jurisdiction) asserts a right for such people to be *included in the territory* governed by the State, assuming no movements of population. The question is: is it also legally conferring a *constitutional* right to *citizenship* of the State for such people? Should that be the case, it does not really lead to any practical change in the current situation, but it does elevate citizenship for those in the six counties from statute to the constitution and therefore any change in this respect henceforth could only come through a referendum rather than just the Dáil. The immediate issue would therefore be in fact one of status and reassurance on citizenship.

Legal views appear divided on the question about the first sentence and citizenship. There are those who say that the wording is at least ambiguous regarding citizenship and others who hold that reference to the "nation", along with the subsequent sentence about being "*otherwise* qualified", ties in sufficiently with "nationality" and "national[s]" in some legal usage to soundly infer entitlement to citizenship for those born in Ireland. All in all, this would indicate that the augmented wording suggested above would have been better and 'for the removal of doubt' if the intention is actually to confer the constitutional right to citizenship that the Taoiseach has signalled in statements. The behaviour of the Irish State authorities since amendment, and not least in regard to immigration, confirms that the official view is that a person born in Ireland is now constitutionally entitled to citizenship.

For its part, the Explanatory Memorandum to the Irish Nationality and Citizenship Bill, 1999, also seemed to indicate that there was now a constitutional right to citizenship in the first sentence of Article 2 as reflected rather than granted in the Bill's S. 3(1)6(1): "Every person born in the island of Ireland is entitled to be an Irish citizen." The Memorandum also said that this took account of the provision of Article 1(vi) of the British-Irish Agreement (accompanying the

---

[6] The socio-cultural unit of the nation can itself have different levels within it ranging from a civic feeling of solidarity to a cultural sense of commonalty. But the point is that any such sense of nationality is more than a category of formal, legal citizenship.

Notes to Chapters

Good Friday Document) whereby the Irish and British Governments undertook to: "recognise the birthright of all the people of Northern Ireland to identify themselves and be accepted as Irish or British, or both, as they may so choose, and accordingly confirm ... their right to hold both British and Irish citizenship ... " Whether or not an ambiguity remains about the locus of this insular right to citizenship (the Constitution or the forthcoming Act [7]) is a matter for juristic debate.

On the point made in the main text about Article 3 and a majority in Ireland for unity relating to "both jurisdictions" rather than "each jurisdiction", this change was crucial. Whether unionists did not spot this or simply did not accept its significance is not clear. As for the new Article 29.7.1, which says that the "State may consent to be bound by the British-Irish Agreement" (which does include an 'each' jurisdiction approach), this does not constitutionally vitiate the point just made. The Agreement is not thus embodied in the Constitution; it is an international accord which the State "may" affirm - but constitutionally it could still have not affirmed it or could now repudiate it or any part of it in certain circumstances.

It would also have been better if the references in Article 3.1 to "unity" and a "united Ireland" in the future had been explicitly linked to sovereign status so as not to be possibly confined to a mere 'hearts and minds' perspective; however, legally, the latter restricted interpretation fortunately would probably not hold up at the end of the day. It should also be noted that while the term "territory" remains in this Article, it is in the sense only of being "shared" by the people of the island, which is nothing like a jurisdictional claim.

It is also interesting to observe that the new Article 3.2 retains a flavour of all-Ireland jurisdiction. In implicitly referring to all-Ireland Implementation Bodies, it permits the exercise of powers on "all or any part of the island" rather than just in "the State".

Finally, if the *State* is now *de jure* as well as *de facto* confined to twenty-six counties for the present (whatever about the *nation* in new Article 2, and the nation's right to sov*ereignty* in extant Article 1), the continuing Article 4 giving "*Ireland*" as the name of the *State* is anomalous. Likewise, the continuing Article 5 in saying: "*Ireland* is a sovereign, independent, democratic *state*." The anomaly is not entirely new, given the usage which developed of referring to the twenty-six counties as the "State". But, in constitutional terms, it

---

[7] The Bill passed through the Seanad and still before the Dáil at time of writing.

could have been argued up to now that Ireland *was de jure* a State, but could only operate *de facto* in twenty-six county terms.[8]

8. UNIONIST QUOTATIONS ON NORTHERN IRELAND ACT 1998

Taken from the House of Commons debates on the Northern Ireland Bill 1998 putting into effect the Good Friday Document.

20/7/98:

Ian Paisley "The Bill seeks to take apart the structures of the Union; it will put Northern Ireland under increasing influence from the south and will exert increasing pressures to destroy the Union."

"All that stands between us and a United Ireland is not legislation in this House but a vote in a poll that will take place when the Secretary of State decides. No elected person in Northern Ireland will have a say about that. The Secretary of State can say, on a whim, 'I shall have a poll, which will be a one-way street. You can vote either to become part of a united Ireland or to remain within the United Kingdom.' No other option will be open."

"Dublin has amended them [Articles 2 and 3] by widening its claim, not on territory but on the people who live in that territory."

R McCartney "It was, and is, necessary to establish a series of institutions under the Bill, the institutions are the north-south ministerial council and the all-Ireland implementation bodies that create, perhaps on the European model, a functionally and factually united Ireland over a period of time. That explains why Sinn Féin-IRA openly expressed the view that the arrangements are transitional. There will come a time when, if such institutions expand, and are dynamic, as proposed in the framework document, Ireland will be factually and functionally united. At that point, the question of consent will arise but consent to what? It will simply be consent that has become either inevitable or unnecessary: a consent to the formal transfer of the legal sovereignty of Northern Ireland to a united Ireland."

J Taylor "Hon. Members talk about the protection provided by the need for consent. There is no protection in that, because the agreement provides for institutions that will circumnavigate such a principle of consent and allow only for a consent to the formal transfer of legal sovereignty. That dichotomy between the institutions

---

[8] 'The People v Ruttledge, 1947', *Irish Reports*, 1978.

Notes to Chapters

required to obtain factual and functional consent and legal sovereignty is also spelled out in that party policy document." [9]

P Robinson "It is very clear that, far from the Bill's leaving Northern Ireland as an integral part of the United Kingdom, it introduces a transitional state. The Bill moves Northern from its full and rightful place within the United Kingdom out on to a limb; it is being pushed towards an all-Ireland state."

"As far as the Union with Ireland Act 1800 [Act of Union] is concerned, the right Hon. Member for Upper Bann [D Trimble] told us at the time of the referendum that it would be unaffected. That was clearly a misleading statement. Clause 2 makes it very clear that the Act is affected: it superseded by this Bill. That is the whole import of clause 2."

J Donaldson "Why does a united Ireland appear to be the only alternative to remaining within the United Kingdom? Could it be that this process is designed gradually to remove Northern Ireland from the United Kingdom?"

"Many share my fear that Irish nationalists hope to use the north-south ministerial council as a means of creating an all-Ireland dimension that will be about the creation of an all-Ireland Government, through the harmonisation of Northern Ireland with the Irish Republic and through the creation of all-Ireland executive bodies. That is what these so-called implementation bodies are: they are all-Ireland executive bodies. They will be given power by this Parliament to exercise power and authority over the whole of the island of Ireland."

"The real reason for the Assembly and the north-south ministerial council being interdependent is so that Unionists will have to acquiesce in the evolution of an all-Ireland Government if they are to retain their positions in the Northern Assembly."

22/7/98:

P Robinson "Under the Bill, the people of Northern Ireland are allowed only to go into a united Ireland or remain in the United Kingdom under the terms of the Bill. They can remain in the United Kingdom not like other citizens, but in a transitional form as they move gently out of the United Kingdom and into a united Ireland ascribed for them in clause 1. Only one option is offered to them in the clause because the whole purpose of the Bill is to lead towards

---

[9] *Towards a United Ireland*, British Labour Party, 1988.

that very option. The Bill's purpose is to take the people of Northern Ireland out of the United Kingdom and into a united Ireland. The provision of clause 1 is to make that come about at the appropriate time."

"The reality is that the Government's policy is based on the premise of the inevitability of a united Ireland. They would not follow the policy that they have at present if they did not believe that that was the direction in which the Province was heading. I do not simply blame the Labour Government for that. They were not the first ones to push down that road. That was the policy being pursued by their predecessors in government."

R McCartney "The reality is that there is a movement to put Northern Ireland out of the United Kingdom. Those of us who oppose the agreement are persuaded that the rationale behind the agreement is to get rid of us - perhaps not overnight, but gradually, over time, to try to persuade the people of Northern Ireland to join the people of the Republic of Ireland."

D Trimble "While it has been the position since 1972-73 that the status could change if there were a vote, the Hon. Member for West Tyrone (Mr. Thompson) made the apt point that up until now all those border polls have been non-binding,

"Clause 1(2) will introduce an obligation on the Secretary of State to make proposals to Parliament to give effect to the results of a referendum."

27/7/98:

W Thompson "We rightly believe that the institution's [North-South Ministerial Council] purpose is to increase and speed up the nationalist desire for a united Ireland and to bring that about in a kind of secret way. ...

"Of course, it is obvious that the council's whole purpose is to try to cushion people and to persuade them that this is the way that they should go."

31/7/98:

P Robinson "The Bill fundamentally weakens the union between Northern Ireland and Great Britain. Anybody with a modicum of sense will recognise that."

Notes to Chapters

3. THE IRISH LEFT

1. THE SOCIAL MARKET

The idea of the social market, but not the term, was promoted by Oskar Lange (1936/7),[10] Polish socialist economist. It continued to be developed up to the Eighties by others - the concept being to combine central planning with demand and allocation of goods and resources being determined by a market mechanism. Sometimes the reference is to 'market socialism' or the 'socialist market'. This outlook has been advocated in a modified way by the British Fabian Society (1986).[11] In some of the later forms, the social market seems not much different from a 'mixed economy' consisting of public and private enterprise in a context of indicative planning.

2. SINN FÉIN - THE OLDEST POLITICAL PARTY

The first Cumann na nGaedheal was founded in 1900 and enunciated the prototype of the Sinn Féin idea. The National Council was launched in 1903 and held its first convention in November 1905 at which the *Sinn Féin Policy* was fully and formally proclaimed. The Sinn Féin League was set up in April 1907 from a merger of Cumann na nGaedheal and the Dungannon Clubs (established March 1905). In August 1907, the Council passed a motion, with overlapping members of the League present and proposing it, to merge with the League. This was confirmed in 1908 with the new body definitely being designated simply as Sinn Féin.

The Ulster Unionist Council (forerunner of the UUP) was mooted in December 1904 and set up in March 1905.

The Labour Party was founded in 1912.

3. VERBAL REPUBLICANISM & FIANNA FÁIL

Even the notorious 'verbal republicanism' of Fianna Fáil seems to be fading fast under Bertie Ahern. After the 1998 referenda (as noted in the main text), he declared on television that the Irish people had at last accepted partition. Later, he suggested that a confederation might be set up in 'these islands' (to be fair, he has not said 'British Isles' - yet). Next, he encouraged consideration of rejoining the Commonwealth. Finally, he renounced his own former

---

[10] Lange, Oskar, 'On the Economic Theory of Socialism', in *Review of Economic Studies*, London, 1936.
[11] Fabian Society, Market Socialism: Whose Choice? A Debate, 1986.

Notes to Chapters

policy of not joining PfP unless there was referendum approval for same which had been advocated in the first place because of the implications for neutrality. He has thus earned his distinctive place in Irish history; however, categorisation of what that is remains another matter

4. SINN FÉIN ELECTORAL RESULTS IN THE TWENTY-SIX COUNTIES

GENERAL ELECTION In the 1997 general election, Sinn Féin went forward in 14 out of 41 constituencies. Its first preference vote as a percentage of the total poll in all 41 was 2.55%. Its average such vote in the 14 constituencies concerned was 7.37%. The results per constituency contested were as follows in descending order:

Cavan-Monaghan	19.37%	Dublin North-East	5.93%
Kerry North	15.91%	Dublin West	5.00%
Dublin South-West	8.90%	Dublin South-Central	4.77%
Louth	8.11%	Cork North-Central	3.76%
Donegal North-East	8.11%	Cork East	3.56%
Sligo-Leitrim	7.10%	Meath	3.53%
Dublin Central	6.65%	Galway West	2.51%

LOCAL ELECTIONS In the 1999 local elections, its first preference vote as an average percentage of the total polls (County Council, Corporation, UDC, TC) was 5.18%. Its first preference vote as an average percentage of all the Local Electoral Areas (equivalent of constituencies) contested was 7.69%. The votes above the latter average were as follows:

County Councils - Monagahan 24.94%, Louth 9.56%, Cavan 8.51%, Leitrim 7.92%, South Dublin 7.78%.

Corporations - Sligo 17.44%, Drogheda 8.42%, Dublin 7.85%.

UDCs - Monaghan 38.79%, Clones 34.2%, Youghal 21.89%, Castleblaney 21.35%, Clonakilty 16.49%, Dundalk 16.26%, Navan 15.91%, Tralee 14.37%, Carrick on Suir 11.59%, Buncrana 9.71%, Carrickmacross 9.67%, Cavan 8.31%.

TCs - Passage West 13.91%, Portlaoise 11.98%, Shannon 9.75%.

EUROPEAN ELECTION - in the 1999 election to the European Parliament, the breakdown of its overall 6.33% first preference vote was as follows per constituency: Dublin 6.64%, Munster 6.48%, Connacht-Ulster 6.39%, Leinster 5.85%.

Notes to Chapters

5. SOCIO-ECONOMIC DEPRIVATION IN IRELAND TODAY

Measurements of poverty are more readily available for the twenty-six counties than the six, although it is unlikely that patterns differ much on either side of the border. The results from a study published in June 1999 revealed that the numbers of people in the twenty-six counties experiencing income poverty was generally higher in 1997 than in 1994.[12] However, there was a decrease in the numbers of people experiencing such poverty together with basic deprivation.

Over one-third of persons fell below the 60% relative income poverty line in 1997, i.e. £94 per week. Over one-fifth were below 50%, i.e. £78 per week. This was an increase of just over 1% in the numbers falling below the corresponding lines in 1994. The proportion of the population on the lowest incomes, below the 40% line (£63 per week), rose from 7% to 10%. Relative income poverty means that a household is getting less than average household income as expressed in the stated percentage terms.

When income poverty was combined with non-monetary indicators of basic deprivation, e.g. not having a warm winter coat or a substantial meal in the day, the overall number of people was lower. Those below the 60% income line and experiencing such deprivation fell from 15% to 10%, while those below the 50% line in a similar situation fell from 9% to 7%. Nevertheless, one-tenth of the population were still in consistent poverty, i.e. the conjunction of income poverty with basic deprivation.

The current overall situation was put in perspective by Garret FitzGerald when he wrote about the Celtic tiger that "this leap in national prosperity has been accompanied by a very evident widening of the gap between the top and bottom ends of the Irish income scale. ... at the bottom of the heap, among the disadvantaged, gains have generally been small and some social problems, such as drug dependency and homelessness, have become notably worse. the failure of our economic and political system to secure a better distribution of the recent huge increase in available resources is extremely disturbing."[13]

---

[12] Callan, T et al, *Monitoring Poverty Trends*, Oak Tree Press, 1999.

[13] 'Opinion', *The Irish Times*, 5/8/00.

Notes to Chapters

4. SOCIAL CLASSES AND POLITICS

1. CORPORATISM

Corporatism was an idea originally invented by Italian fascism as a means of superseding class consciousness and politics. Workers were instead to see themselves as members of a corporation, or firm or industry, in a collaborative exercise with managers and employers, and behave accordingly. The idea has been modified by some since then whereby society has become the 'corporation'; the expressions 'partnership' and 'social partners' can on occasion also be used to suggest this. While one does not have to subscribe to the notion of perpetual class war to defend the distinctive interests of employees, corporatism, in its playing down of different interests, is definitely skewed towards the establishment

2. THE PROGRESSIVE CLASSES IN IRELAND

Measuring the progressive classes presents both conceptual and statistical problems. The latter is especially the case when having to use different kinds of censuses for north and south and at different dates. Even when there is a clear idea of whom it is desired to include in the group, there are difficulties about the composition of census categories and then about making the data comparable. However, for our purposes of socio-political assessment, it is not felt that these distortions are significant. Indeed, one may assume that they lead to somewhat understating the strength of the 'progressive classes'.

In this instance, for the south, in the last census of 1996 we took, under "socio-economic group" and for "persons aged 15 years and over in the labour force", the categories Own Account, Unskilled, Semi-skilled, Manual Skilled, Non-manual, and Lower Professional.[14] Some of those in Higher Professional would be likely to fall within the scope of the 'progressive classes', but it was not possible to numerically extract them (e.g. "social workers and probation officers"). For the north, in the last census of 1991 we took, under "socio-economic groups" and for the "population aged 16 years and over" who were "economically active", the categories Own Account Other than Professional, Unskilled Manual, Semi-skilled Manual, Skilled Manual, Foremen and Supervisors - Manual, Personal Service Workers, Junior Non-manual, Foremen and Supervisors - Non-

---

[14] *Census 96, Volume 7, Occupations*, CSO, 1998.

Notes to Chapters

manual, Ancillary Workers and Artists, and Professional Workers - Employees.[15] Sections of the armed forces had to be included in the southern figures, but could be and were excluded in the northern ones; however, this seemed appropriate enough for obvious reasons.

The outcome of this exercise was to give data as follows: 1,099,437 (south), 476,146 (north) and, therefore, 1,575,583 (all-Ireland). In a combined labour force of 2,215,984, that would give just over 71% for the progressive classes.

If agricultural workers were included, the figure would of course be greater, but not significantly at almost 73%, given the extent to which this category of worker has declined in the face of farm technology and as the agricultural community has become preponderantly self-employed

As for the long-term unemployed, the nearest measure we have is the number out of work on the island for "one year or more" of which there were 60,010 at the end of 1999 in a total unemployment pool of 137,700 according to the criteria of the International Labour Organisation.[16]

5. THE INTERNATIONAL CONTEXT

1. THE 'THIRD WORLD'

The 'Third World' signifies the underdeveloped countries between the developed 'First' of the capitalist West and the developed 'Second' of the communist East; it may be a bit of a misnomer now that the latter has collapsed, and with Asian tigers around, but the reference endures as a term of convenience.

2. SMALL BUSINESS & THE EU

Garret FitzGerald once argued that the EU should not just be seen as a bourgeois capitalist project, given the resistance to it shown by several sections of business as manifest in many chambers of

---

[15] *The Northern Ireland Census 1991 - Economic Activity Report*, Belfast HMSO, 1993.

[16] *Quarterly National Household Survey - 4th Quarter*, CSO, 2000 & *Labour Force Survey - Quarterly Supplement Sept-Nov '99*, Belfast HMSO, 2000. ILO unemployment figures should not be confused with numbers on the Live Register which include part-timers, casual workers etc and even housewives in certain instances; for example, the number on the Register for the twenty-six counties alone in November '99 was 178,600.

commerce. But the suggestion of the Left is not that there was no opposition from *small* capital to the designs of big capital.

6. MODERN REPUBLICANISM

1. 'SOCIAL REPUBLICANISM'

The term 'social republicanism' is used, particularly by some anti-nationalists, to denote the taking up of social and economic issues by republicans as a means of garnering support for the cause of a sovereign all-Ireland republic. It has been applied to Liam Mellows, the Republican Congress of 1934 and the 'official' republican tendency of the Sixties and Seventies. In other words, the issues concerned are seen as being used in an opportunistic way rather than as proceeding from republican philosophy, and the phenomenon as arising historically and politically when republicanism is arrested in its progress otherwise. A distinction is drawn between this and the Connolly tradition of socialist republicanism which is viewed as beginning instead with socialism and then concluding that a republic is necessary in order to achieve socialist objectives.

It is probably true that there have been and are some republicans of limited ideological outlook whom 'social republicanism', as defined, describes accurately. However, to say that when republicans emphasise social and economic grievances, it is always as an add-on is inaccurate. The fact is that republicanism originates in the mass of the people and it is only natural that, if one thinks through what the content of a republic should be, social and economic matters have to be addressed and as they affect the ordinary person. Moreover, insofar as republicanism is about freedom, it begs the question of how far emancipation can be taken at all levels, which inevitably points in a progressive direction. Although not all republicans will agree that that requires socialism. But, yet again, that depends on what is meant by socialism. Clearly what is also important is the main class base of republicanism and, in current circumstances, that would reinforce the interpretation that social and economic change is inextricably linked into the republican project and not some contingent or dispensable item.

2. ETHNICITY

It should be understood that 'ethnic' comes from Greek 'ethnos' for 'nation', but tends to be used on occasion in connection with 'race', which is 'genos' in Greek, but with no adjectival equivalent of 'ethnic' in English; 'genic' has got to do instead with 'genes'.

Notes to Chapters

3. GLOCALISATION

The pressures of globalisation in economics and communication. can induce re-appreciations of the importance of roots and control over one's environment. These re-appreciations then ironically use the novelties of modern technology (the internet etc) both to enable the nation to articulate itself to itself as well as to the world, and to link up with people in other nations to share experiences of endurance and renewal. Glocalisation is a term used to describe this kind of phenomenon.

4. REPUBLICANISM & NATIONALISM: AN IMAGINED CONFLICT

[The following is the main content of a memorandum produced in August 2000 in reaction to the article specified below.]

The Ireland Institute has taken a worthy initiative in launching a new magazine entitled *The Republic*.[17] Ironically, however, the introductory article, 'Beyond Nationalism: Time to Reclaim the Republican Ideal', is counter-productive from a republican standpoint insofar as that aims to advance to the fullest extent the rights of the Irish nation and of its citizenry.

The article commences with a statement of the need to undo the "confusion of republicanism with nationalism". What ensues is an imagined conflict between the two positions rather than a clarification of content and compatibility. The source of the difficulty is established early on by rejecting the approach of "nationalisms", or put less academically, denying the fact that there are different kinds of nationalism.

As an ideology, nationalism generally emerged in modern history in the form of movements against empire through the assertion that nations have the right to independence.[18] (Later, they would be alternatively described as anti-imperialist, although that epithet can be attached to other and complementary stances as well.[19]) The nation was defined in terms of a socio-cultural entity, although with various mixes and emphases ranging from the heterogeneity of the

---

[17] No. 1, Dublin, June 2000.

[18] Although an independent nation state logically need not be internally democratic or liberal, nationalist movements tended to embody these perspectives.

[19] For example, persons in metropolitan countries opposing their own nation's expansionism.

Swiss to the virtual homogeneity of the Hungarians, to take but two examples. In other words, the movements in question were not just civic in being comprised of citizens or those thus seeking citizenship instead of subjecthood; they were also ethnic in the delineation of the particular groups of citizens or would-be citizens concerned - therefore the description nationalist.[20]

But, while all nationalists hold that the nation should be self-governing, in respect of *how* it should be so, there *are* of course varieties of nationalism, just as there are of conservatism, liberalism and socialism. On the right, there is fundamentalist and conservative nationalism; on the left, liberal and socialist nationalism. In Irish circumstances, the fundamentalist would insist on a Catholic nation, while the conservative wants laissez-faire economics and has a narrow perspective on civil liberties; the liberal is more flexible on the economic front but is safe on civil liberties, while the socialist is also secure on the latter and advocates democracy throughout the socio-economic system.

It is this refusal to accept that there are varieties of nationalism which leads to the blanket statement that: "Nationalism categorises the world only in terms of nation and nationality. It ignores other categories such as gender, ethnicity, sexuality, class and more." True of some nationalists, perhaps, but not of others. Following on from this, it is averred: "If there is a conflict based on gender or class, in what way can an appeal to nationality as arbiter resolve that conflict? The only answer it can find is one which is already contained within the nation, and it is this which inclines nationalism towards conservative and authoritarian solutions and a propensity to favour the powerful and privileged." The fact that some nationalists ally the drive for national freedom with a commitment to domestic change is overlooked. Next, we hear that: "Culture from outside the nation will seem alien and to some degree will be interpreted as threatening to the national culture." Again, true of *some* nationalists. Apart from that, shades of the old and spurious opposition of nationalism versus internationalism (repeated elsewhere) when in reality they can be two sides of the same coin: for instance, in cul-

---

[20] However, 'colonial nationalism' did not include aboriginal peoples, and certain examples of 'internal colonialism' can be found elsewhere. For example, some of the south Slavs fighting with the Hungarians against the Austrians in the mid 19th century switched sides when they found out that the borders of the old Hungary were to be maintained and would still incorporate them.

ture, treasure quality in your own and augment it with quality from others. At the same time, if external culture is that of an imperial power and being imposed on a nation while that nation's culture is being extirpated, resistance to attempted substitution, as distinct from worthwhile addition, is only natural.

The article may also be the victim of its own abstract categories. Insofar as national*ism* is to be defined as dealing only with the national aspect of things, that does not mean that the national*ist*, when confronted with certain problems, refers just to the nation for their solution. But even this distinction is somewhat limiting; not infrequently, the nationalist wants to be self-governing precisely for the purpose of changing some things within the nation - e.g. nationalism with a view to modernism! Or put yet another way, nationalism can not only sit easily alongside domestic transformation, sometimes it is seen as a necessary condition for its achievement. Such national*ism* is *not*, therefore, defined merely by the national *as it is*, but also by how it can and *ought to be*. These considerations are where the varieties identified above come in.[21]

"Nationalism, it is argued, is simultaneously liberating and oppressive, cosmopolitan and chauvinistic, democratic and undemocratic. The usefulness of a concept which can contain such opposing meanings at the one time is doubtful." Here, there is reference not only to the blurring of distinctions among different sorts of nationalism in regard to the objects of independence, but also to the blurring of the contrast between imperialism (or colonialism) and nationalism insofar as the first often rests on the alleged superiority of one nation over another or others. But this may be said to be not primarily a conceptual so much as a terminological dilemma (and not altogether a contingent one) of which more below.

Not surprisingly, given what has gone before, the article proceeds as follows:

" ... while nationalism offers a convenient unifying point, its programme of building a nation state is essentially conservative and runs counter to the other transformative trends. Ironically, the nationalist part of the [national][22] movement [!] proposes to build a state which is the mirror image of what the struggle is against: it is only the nationality of the state which will be different."

---

[21] This has been particularly so in the case of some African and Asian nationalist movements.

[22] As the movement is defined in the preceding sentence.

Reconstructed in a more precise political fashion, it might run like this (note emphases):

"... while nationalism offers a convenient unifying point, *a programme for some* of building a nation state is essentially conservative and runs counter to the other transformative trends. [Not "Ironically"] the *right-wing* part of the *nationalist* movement proposes to build a state which is *in its socio-economic character* the mirror image of what the struggle *by left-wing nationalists* is against: it is only the nationality of the state which will be different."

And, one might add, the persons who govern it. Also, it is declared: "Neither democracy nor the republic refer to the nation or nationality." That may be so semantically, but how are they to be made politically concrete other than by resting on the nation? Or are we back to Austro-Marxism with its hope of transmogrifying an empire into a republic with whatever contemporary equivalent is chosen - the EU perhaps?

We are next informed that: "Attaching rights and obligations to a common citizenship leads to more open and democratic outcomes than attaching them to nationality." Once more, false antithesis raises its head. There is no necessary 'either/or' here. One has rights both as a member of a nation and as a citizen and the two cannot be divorced if democracy is to be fulfilled in the real world. One has rights as an *Irish* citizen or as a *French* citizen, and so on. Some of these rights are human and universal (freedom of conscience), others are more particular (use of a specific language).[23] Another illustration of sweeping false antithesis is the following: "The right of the nation to be self-governing is placed above the right of each person to be self-governing, and the welfare of the nation, which usually means the interests of the dominant section." This might describe the position of Griffith; it certainly would not that of Connolly. There is then the conclusion: "While republicanism rejects the idea that nation and nationality should be the basis for political organisation, or that nation should be equated

---

[23] If there is a tension between the civic and the ethnic in Ireland today, the real one is clearly between unionism/loyalism and nationalism/republicanism, at least in terms of community and identity, requiring, among other things, confirmation that fidelity to Reformation Protestantism does not demand union with Britain and attachment to Tridentine Catholicism is not a condition of Irish independence. Otherwise, the cultural content of Irishness in the civic-ethnic continuum should be a matter of choice.

with the state, it does respect and welcome them as forms of community and identity." One wonders where this leaves the United Nations and its premise of self-determination? Of course, nations and states, given geographic and demographic factors, cannot always be congruent, even after self-determination, and the rights of national minorities, where they exist, should be respected. But that does not take away from the fact that, in the modern world, the nation is the principal determinant of the state. To some extent, it depends here on what is meant by "political organisation" and being "equated with the state". Insofar as it is a protest against forced homogeneity and intolerance, that is unobjectionable. However, as it stands, the statement perpetuates the failure to distinguish between the approaches of right and left-wing nationalism.

It is true that, whatever about its origins, nationalism as a term has by now unfortunately, owing to sloppy usage in both academia and journalism, become convoluted for many in its general significance. This is not entirely accidental. If, in *international* relations, for instance, the nation is taken, on the one hand, in an egalitarian way as a justification for independence and, on the other, in a superior way for domination, and 'nationalism' is used to describe both situations, then meaning is blunted and has to be qualified by referring to democratic or aggressive nationalism.[24] (Previously, the first would have simply been nationalism and the second imperialism.) It may be that, in global political discourse, such a point of required qualification has been reached. But let us at least acknowledge that and not persist in the obfuscation that there is only one 'nationalism', either domestically or in international relations. An excellent example in international relations of convenient obfuscation was when Britain attacked Egypt in 1956 and said it was standing up to nationalism in much the same way as it had stood up to Hitler!

We must also be conscious of a usage deriving specifically from Irish history. With capital initials, Nationalism and Republicanism came to have respectively right and left-wing connotations, because, more laterally, of the Redmond-Griffith and Pearse-Connolly spectra. But the nomenclature of parties or constellations of same should not bedevil political analysis. The fact is that Redmond was a home rule nationalist, Griffith a duo-monarchical nationalist, Pearse a democratic republican nationalist, and Connolly a socialist

---

[24] That is apart from fundamentalist/conservative and liberal/socialist 'nationalisms' all of which are at least anti-colonialist (although some would say not all are anti-neocolonialist).

republican nationalist. However, the nationalist-republican dichotomy of nomenclature was perpetuated in the partitioned six counties with the continued existence of a Nationalist Party and the alternative of the Republican Movement. Yet, properly speaking, in Ireland all republicans were nationalist, even if not all nationalists were republican. (One suspects that the article is significantly influenced by this dichotomy and also by a certain ultra-leftist dogmatism.)

Subsequent to 1921, however, every form of Irish nationalism in time became in effect republican, if only with a small 'r', because being a nationalist region or co-player in empire was no longer an option, and nobody seriously suggested that an independent Ireland should be a monarchy in its own right rather than some kind of republic, whether or not the word was to be used in the official title of the State. Currently, SDLP politicians are wont on occasion to stress that they are republican as well as nationalist. (In the contest for support that is taking place in the north, the intelligent riposte for SF would be to underline that it is nationalist as well as republican.)

Moreover, if there is a contemporary broader *terminological* problem with nationalism, republicanism is not without its difficulties either. We have referred to the classical denotation of nationalism and agree, in the same classical vein, that "a republic without democracy would not be a republic", that it has got to do with "the welfare of the people" and that it enshrines the principles of "liberty, equality and fraternity". But how many 'republics' are or have been capable of such attribution? And what about some 'republicans', whether those in the US or the neo-fascist republikaner in Germany? Is it any surprise that people now also talk about *democratic* republics (even in official title) and conservative and radical republicans? Republic now often just conveys that the head of state is not a monarch, although he or she may be the vilest of dictators. Does that beg the challenge that we must seek to recover the original and essentially progressive nature of republicanism? Is there not then also the challenge of recovering the original and essentially progressive nature of nationalism?[25]

---

[25] At the same time, this is more of a problem in international debate because, while that can feed back into discussion on this island (as the article in question demonstrates), generally speaking, Irish people do not find in nationalism a suggestion of fascism or view republicanism as a neutral description when it comes to consideration of the radical.

Notes to Chapters

In that sense, if republicanism and nationalism are to be compared, we should be explaining where they overlap and combine to eventuate in the enlightened result of a national republic.[26] The ideological struggle here is not *between* nationalism and republicanism, but *within* each and to produce the best of both; we don't want nationalism without meaningful democratic content, and we don't want republicanism without meaningful social content.[27] Counterposition of nationalism and republicanism instead of selective synthesis is the real confusion and one which can only be damaging to advanced politics in the north in particular and throughout the island in general.

---

[26] Connolly warned against "Nationalism without Socialism", just as he was opposed to nationalism without republicanism. But it was not a case of socialism *instead* of nationalism anymore than of republicanism *instead* of nationalism. (*Socialism and Nationalism*, D Ryan [ed], Three Candles, 1948.)

[27] One could add that a specific task is getting militar*ism* out of republicanism and hibernianism out of both.